How to Handle False Prophets and False Prophecies

Michael Rhoads

WESTBOW
PRESS
A DIVISION OF THOMAS NELSON

WestBow Press books may be ordered through
booksellers or by contacting:

WestBow Press
A Division of Thomas Nelson
1663 Liberty Drive
Bloomington, IN 47403
www.westbowpress.com
1-(866) 928-1240

ISBN: 978-1-4497-8723-3 (sc)
ISBN: 978-1-4497-8724-0 (e)

Library of Congress Control Number: 2013904035

Printed in the United States of America

WestBow Press rev. date: 3/22/2013

How to Handle False Prophets and False Prophecies - Description of Hebrew names

It is my personal belief that we need to preserve the holiness of Abba's name and of His Son's name. Below are the Hebrew names and the corresponding English phonetic pronunciation with how they appear in English Bibles to help you when you read this book.

יְהוָה אֲדֹנָי Adonai Yahweh – LORD God

אֱלֹהִים Eloheem – God (includes all 3 – Father, Son and Holy Spirit)

יְהוָה צְבָאוֹת - Yahweh Tzebaot – Lord of hosts

יֵשׁוּעַ - Yahshua (Jesus Christ of Nazareth)

אֱלֹהֶיךָ – YOUR GOD

Exd 20:7

"You shall not take the name of אֱלֹהֶיךָ יְהוָה in vain, for יְהוָה will not hold [him] guiltless who takes His name in vain.

Remember the 10 commandments!

1

HOW TO HANDLE FALSE PROPHETS and False Prophecies – Michael Rhoads

....BEWARE - they come as innocent as lambs, but inwardly they are FEROCIOUS WOLVES. (Jesus Christ of Nazareth - who I call by His Hebrew name -Yahshua יְשׁוּעַ) warned us. As one with a heart to set people free from ALL deception, not just deceiving spirits that forbid food and marriage in the last days (1 Timothy 4), but also FALSE PROPHECY, I have attracted quite a few people who have falsely prophesied or are FALSE PROPHETS.

Remember, we are to pray for the gift of prophecy. Even to EARNESTLY desire the gift (1 Cor. 14). We are also commanded to JUDGE prophecy.

1Th 5:21

Test all things; hold fast what is good.

In other words, do not just RECEIVE all that is said to you by someone who seems spiritual. I found myself needing to become increasingly more discerning of "prophets" who are very critical and quick to find fault with others. Many prophetically gifted people are insecure and feel the need to be "control freaks" (myself included). This is not operation of His gift - it is ABUSE of His gift. So be careful of this MIX of flesh and spirit that goes on a lot in the last days. Do not mix TRUE prophecy of His words with fleshly attempts to control others that are rooted in jealousy, demonic wisdom (James 3) and insecurity.

Some of the most vicious false prophet (-esses) have been hurt very deeply, as have some of the most powerful TRUE prophets. I believe Abba ALLOWS this because it gives prophetic people an EDGE that NORMAL people do not have. I have a friend whose brother tried to kill him, then killed himself and my friend was clinically dead and went to heaven. I try not to miss a meeting with him, because now he has revelations about heaven and Abba reveals many deep things to him! There is a saying that a prophetic life is a lonely life, and I see this to be true. Think of Jeremiah - he was not even allowed to go to birthday parties! Abba had a HIGHER calling on this man's life. Some prophetic people I know do not watch ANY TV, celebrate Christmas, do not mess around with many material possessions, and so on. BUT THIS DOES NOT MEAN THAT WEAKER CHRISTIANS NEED TO JUDGE, AND IT DOES NOT MEAN THAT PROPHETIC PEOPLE NEED TO JUDGE THE LESS SPIRITUAL. This is where compassion comes in, and in trying to help a person who says they hear His voice, we need to be also broken for them and the area of heartbreak they are struggling with. For example, I met a homeless man, recently in Brooklyn. I KNOW he had the Holy Spirit, but he insisted that Abba had sent him to sleep on the sidewalk because it was his post, as a soldier of Messiah. He would NOT accept offers to stay in a better place, even if church people made them. ???

People who prophesy out of their hearts, are prophesying out of the wrong place. Prophecy comes out of your spirit, not your heart, and it is FOR BELIEVERS. As beautiful of a voice as Celine Dion has, she sings OUT OF HER HEART, and to my knowledge is NOT born again. So do not even TRY to say that the Holy Spirit was prophesying to you through one of her songs, or Madonna or some other ridiculous FALSE PROPHET who has a pretty voice. What did Abba tell Ezekiel?

"Son of man, prophesy against the prophets of Israel who prophesy, and say to those who prophesy out of their own heart, 'Hear the word of יְהוָֹה אֲדֹ֒נָי!' "

Eze 13:3

Thus says יְהוָֹה אֲדֹ֒נָי: "Woe to the foolish prophets, who follow their own spirit and have seen nothing

Eze 13:4

"O Israel, your prophets are like foxes in the deserts.

Eze 13:5

"You have not gone up into the gaps to build a wall for the house of Israel to stand in battle on the day of יְהוָֹה אֲדֹ֒נָי

Eze 13:6

"They have envisioned futility and false divination, saying, 'Thus says יְהוָֹה אֲדֹ֒נָי!' But יְהוָֹה אֲדֹ֒נָי has not sent them; yet they hope that the word may be confirmed.

Eze 13:7

"Have you not seen a futile vision, and have you not spoken false divination? You say, ' יְהוָֹה אֲדֹ֒נָי says,' but I have not spoken."

5

Eze 13:8

Therefore thus says יְהוִה אֲדֹנָי: "Because you have spoken nonsense and envisioned lies, therefore I [am] indeed against you," says יְהוִה אֲדֹנָי.

In my early days in Christ, when I was coming into the revelation about the gifts of the Spirit, I was SO EXCITED to prophesy, that I actually said some "prophecies" that did not come to pass. Did this make me a "false prophet"? Absolutely NOT! I was immature and overzealous. I had to grow in my gift, and use it to build up, comfort and exhort the body of Christ! I also needed to grow in the fear of יְהוִה אֲדֹנָי In fact, read what the torah says:

If there arises among you a prophet or a dreamer of dreams, and he gives you a sign or a wonder,

Deu 13:2

"and the sign or the wonder comes to pass, that he spoke to you, saying, 'Let us go after other gods'--that you have not known--'and let us serve them,'

Deu 13:3

"you shall not listen to the words of that prophet or that dreamer of dreams, for אֱלֹהֵיכֶם יְהוָה is testing you to know whether you love אֱלֹהֵיכֶם יְהוָה with all your heart and with all your soul.

Deu 13:4

"You shall walk after אֶל יְהוָה אֱלֹהֵיכֶם and fear Him, and keep His commandments and obey His voice; you shall serve Him and hold fast to Him.

Deu 13:5

"But that prophet or that dreamer of dreams shall be put to death, because he has spoken in order to turn [you] away from אֶל יְהוָה אֱלֹהֵיכֶם, who brought you out of the land of Egypt and redeemed you from the house of bondage, to entice you from the way that אֶל יְהוָה אֱלֹהֵיכֶם commanded you to walk. So you shall put away the evil from your midst.

Deu 13:6

"If your brother, the son of your mother, your son or your daughter, the wife of your bosom, or your friend who is as your own soul, secretly entices you, saying, 'Let us go and serve other gods,' which you have not known, neither you nor your fathers...notice that the sign or wonder comes to pass! But then the "prophet" leads you into worship of another god...These are the prophets you need to watch out for!

The prophet who has a dream, let Him tell a dream; And he who has My word, let him speak My word faithfully. What [is] the chaff to the wheat?" says יְהוָה צְבָא וֹת.

Jer 23:29

"[Is] not My word like a fire?" says יְהוָה צְבָא וֹת, "And like a hammer [that] breaks the rock in pieces?

Jer 23:30

7

"Therefore behold, I [am] against the prophets," says צְבָא וֹת יְהֹוָה, "who steal My words every one from his neighbor.

Jer 23:31 "Behold, I [am] against the prophets," says צְבָא וֹת יְהֹוָה, "who use their tongues and say, 'He says.'

Jer 23:32

"Behold, I [am] against those who prophesy false dreams," says יְהֹוָה צְבָא וֹת, "and tell them, and cause My people to err by their lies and by their recklessness. Yet I did not send them or command them; therefore they shall not profit this people at all," says יְהֹוָה צְבָא וֹת.

Jer 23:33

"So when these people or the prophet or the priest ask you, saying, 'What is the oracle of יְהֹוָה צְבָא וֹת ' you shall then say to them, 'What oracle?' I will even forsake you," says צְבָא וֹת יְהֹוָה.

Jer 23:34

"And [as for] the prophet and the priest and the people who say, 'The oracle of יְהֹוָה צְבָא וֹת !' I will even punish that man and his house.

So, יְהֹוָה צְבָא וֹת spoke to Jeremiah AND Moses (both TRUE prophets) and warned about 2 things - DREAMS and people who put words into the mouth of יְהֹוָה צְבָא וֹת as a way of trying to control others.

8

It was VERY irritating when I was a pre-school teacher, and my students would say, "Mr. Michael said," to try and manipulate other students or impose their will and force their way, when I had NOT said that. יְהֹוָה צְבָאֹות also hates this! It is better to offer your opinion and to just leave יְהֹוָה צְבָאֹות OUT OF IT! Do not use Him or His name to try and force your will on others - that is more like witchcraft and how the occult operates ... let me give a few examples of REALLY CONFUSING "prophecies"

1-A girl once told me that יְהֹוָה צְבָאֹות told HER to do a backbend

2-A single mother once told me that יְהֹוָה צְבָאֹות TOLD HER that I was her husband. She then threatened to commit suicide if I did not marry her (by the way, I DID NOT MARRY HER....)

3-A very old widow once told me that יְהֹוָה צְבָאֹות said she had to move a shelf in her house. SHE ALMOST KILLED HERSELF BY PULLING THE THING ON TOP OF HERSELF!!! (SHE WAS CONVINCED THAT ANY TIME THE CITY AUTHORITIES TOLD HER TO DO SOMETHING, IT WAS יְהֹוָה צְבָאֹות).

The last woman, I tried to tell her with all due respect NOT TO say "HE SAID" something that He did not! The city government is VERY FAR from being the voice of אֱלֹהִים!

I LOVE women - do not get me wrong (I am married to one) - but Paul made it VERY clear about women prophesying, that they need a COVERING (1 Cor. 11). A man with discernment needs to be there helping the woman. Women are more open to deception by "lying signs and wonders" that are to be prominent in the last days. Think of Eve!

The coming of the [lawless one] is according to the working of Satan, with all power, signs, and lying wonders,

2Th 2:10

and with all unrighteous deception among those who perish, because they did not receive the love of the truth, that they might be saved.

A pastor once showed me FAKE and REAL money. They are hard to distinguish! We need discernment because we can greatly benefit from the TRUE use of TRUE prophetic gifts in the body of Christ. TRUE prophets will not cause people to forget Abba's true name:

"I have heard what the prophets have said who prophesy lies in My name, saying, 'I have dreamed, I have dreamed!'

Jer 23:26

"How long will [this] be in the heart of the prophets who prophesy lies? Indeed [they are] prophets of the deceit of their own heart,

Jer 23:27

"who try to make My people forget My name by their dreams that everyone tells his neighbor, as their fathers forgot My name for Baal.

The spirit of Balaam and Jezebel are RAMPANT in the last days, so BE CAREFUL. I once saw on a YouTube video a popular Christian artist claim that she saw אֱלֹהִים – if this is true, how is she still alive?

Jdg 13:22 And **Manoah** said to his wife, "We shall surely die, because we have seen אֱלֹהִים!"

Jhn 1:18

No one has seen אֱלֹהִים at any time. The only begotten Son, who is in the bosom of the Father, He has declared [Him].

1Jo 4:12No one has seen אֱלֹהִים at any time. If we love one another, אֱלֹהִים abides in us, and His love has been perfected in us.

A prophecy was made this year that Abba is going to be doing some SHEEP GOAT separating and it's not going to be pretty. Imagine - your head pastor being exposed as actually a GOAT who does not even know the Father! Or the Son! So - saints, in times when there is GREAT WICKEDNESS, the righteous go into HIDING. So, if you are hungry, does this "prophet" feed you?

Thirsty? Give you drink?

Naked? Clothe you...

Sick or in prison? how does this "prophet" respond to human need? That is the difference between sheep and goats. I have heard many people SCREAM and SING and QUOTE SCRIPTURE perfectly, but the great test of TIME exposed that they were themselves thorny ground hearers, choked by deceitfulness of riches...

Also, the homosexual spirit is rampant in the last days. People seem to be enamored that they are the BRIDE of Christ (men), and I have heard major pastors of HUGE churches make JOKES about homosexuality - from the pulpit! They do not realize how destructive these jokes are, nor the floodgate they are opening for that spirit to infest their church through them. My friend went on a "mission trip" with a false prophet a few years ago to the Dominican Republic, and to my horror, this man was exposed as a child molester and ended up in jail!! BUT HIS PROPHECIES WERE RIGHT ON! He even said something to me to try and twist my mind that, had I not been spiritually discerning, I could have fell for his trap in my hunger for spiritual truth when I was around 21. The homosexual spirit is an unclean spirit that John saw in the book of Revelation...

And I saw three unclean spirits like frogs [coming] out of the mouth of the dragon, out of the mouth of the beast, and out of the mouth of the false prophet.

Rev 16:14

For they are spirits of demons, performing signs, that go out to the kings of the earth and of the whole world, to gather them to the battle of that great day אֵל שַׁדַּי.

Rev 16:15

"Behold, I am coming as a thief. Blessed [is] he who watches, and keeps his garments, lest he walk naked and they see his shame."

I believe the church in America is in GRAVE danger. The ones that are NOT all the way asleep spiritually are CLOSE. Though I was blessed to be a part of some revival, specifically in the Kansas City area, the spirit of false prophecy seems to be so strong and people seem to be so deceived, that I do not know whether to RUN and HIDE, until the destruction passes by, or to FIGHT. ANY SUGGESTIONS!!??

Discern between prophetic words and words of knowledge. A word of knowledge comes usually to people who are doing evangelism, but also to people with the gift of healing. A prophetic word is giving to edify, comfort and / or exhort people in the body of Christ. Just because someone feels like they heard the voice of the Shepherd, does not always mean that they did. So, before you go broadcasting your "word," make sure

1. Women that you are covered by a pastor, your husband, or your dad. realize that you are opposing the work of Christ by giving messages from Him that are actually NOT and the judgment on false prophets I believe is SEVERE. I once was seeking Him in the wilderness in a season when I was teaching young people, and I saw a vision of a fireball consume me ENTIRELY on an altar. While I thought this may have been Holy Spirit fire, I was also sternly warned by the Father - this was a judgment for FALSE PROPHETS, and I needed to use my gift on young

people with FEAR and TREMBLING. Do you know how many young people have been led astray and into psychotic behaviors by "prophecies" that were made about who they were supposed to be married to???

2. Men that you REALLY make sure it was Him. Ask yourself, "If I give this word, will it EDIFY (build up), COMFORT (perhaps a lonely widow or a homeless person) and / or EXHORT?" Let me also explain exhortation. Disobedience to exhortation is not always SIN. For example, once I was out sharing the gospel at a shopping mall. The Holy Spirit said, through a woman, "please do not leave." I could discern it was not really her speaking - it was the Spirit of Yah MANIFESTING through her. This exhortation was to make sure I was willing to keep sharing, but it would not have been SIN for me not to have obeyed. (The Holy Spirit understands work schedules!) Exhortation is good with fasting too. For example, if I found out someone was fasting, and wanted to exhort them to keep going, I may say, "Can you take my homeless friend into your place for a few nights"? (Read Isaiah 58 if you are wondering what that has to do with fasting.) That is an EXHORTATION. It would not be a sin for the person to NOT do that (?) but it would GREATLY please the Father and perhaps a blessing would be missed if the opportunity was not taken advantage of.

Prophecy is many times BLACK and WHITE. There are NO GREY areas with prophecy. It is a LAST CHANCE effort by יְהֹוָה צְבָא ֹ ות to reach people.

What to do if you made a false prophecy:

First of all, do not beat yourself up! There is NORomas condemnation for those who are in Messiah Yahshua יֵשׁוּעַ (Romans 8).

Like any other sin, REPENT, put it under the blood, apologize if you made a mistake, and MOVE ON! Ask יְהוָה צְבָאוֹת for more grace and mercy to use your gift for Him!

One summer, I gave a prophecy about an earthquake happening before that summer was over. Feeling discouraged, because the summer was almost over, and there had been no earthquake, I was ready to QUIT! (By the way, I found out about 3 days before summer ended that the earthquake hit and its epicenter was almost EXACTLY where I had received the prophecy.)

At the Feast of Tabernacles, in Jerusalem in 2010, I made a prophecy about 3 blasphemers of the Spirit of יְהוָה צְבָאוֹת being CUT OFF in the life of myself, Baruch the best man from my Jerusalem wedding and Anni before the Feast 2011. We found out that that Muslim King in Afghanistan (? I think) was killed by the US armed forces less than one year later. I did not realize this man had blasphemed the Spirit!

The fruit of a good prophecy is - DOES IT COME TO PASS and IS THE BODY OF CHRIST EDIFIED AND COMFORTED AND EXHORTED THROUGH IT? The fruit of a BAD prophecy is

does the person lead people to worship other gods?

and DID THIS PERSON DENY Yahshua יֵשׁוּעַ as the WORD who was made flesh and dwelt among us...?

In Tel Aviv, there was a man with an evil spirit (or many) who spoke "prophecies" through that demon. He would sit on a blanket and say he was Jesus and he usually had food and some zombie-like women around him. He slithered like a snake, BUT PEOPLE WERE DRAWN TO HIM! When we went there, I yelled at him (maybe unwise - but I HATE false prophecy). Then, an amazing thing happened - when we fasted and prayed and went back, prayer walking around that area, יְהֹוָה צְבָא וֹת gave us a WORD -

Zec 13:2

"It shall be in that day," says יְהֹוָה צְבָא וֹת, "[that] I will cut off the names of the idols from the land, and they shall no longer be remembered. I will also cause the prophets and the unclean spirit to depart from the land.

After we prayed that word over the area, we went back and FOUND THAT HE WAS NOWHERE TO BE FOUND! So, we can trust יְהֹוָה צְבָא וֹת to do what He says! So do not be afraid of false prophets! He is in control of the "spirits of the prophets"

1Cr 14:32

And the spirits of the prophets are subject to the prophets.

Prophetic advancement. Often יְהֹוָה צְבָא וֹת will give you an exhortation, and my experience is that you remain at that level of your spiritual walk until YOU keep your end of the deal.

When you obey, He will increase revelation and give MORE. Prophecy is like a puzzle that unfolds, step by step, piece by piece. I have spoken with so many evangelists who were feeling condemnation because they were feeling exhortation to share the gospel with someone and were afraid. DO NOT LET THE ENEMY BEAT YOU UP OVER THIS!

What I have noticed personally in evangelism is that when יְהוָה צְבָאˈות leads me to talk to someone, and if I do not, HE OFTEN GIVES ME THAT ALMOST EXACT SAME SCENARIO AGAIN! It's almost like a test. Once, I was taking my wife to the dentist, and while she was there, I was going to share the gospel. I noticed 4 youths who Anni even said were probably good for me to talk to. Trying to be a gentleman, I walked her up to the dentist office and then walked back down, thinking I would talk to them. THEY WERE ALREADY GONE!

NO!! I thought I failed יְהוָה צְבָאˈות BUT THAT WAS THE ENEMY BRINGING CONDEMNATION! Would you believe, later, at the cafe, as we were sitting and fellowshipping, I LOOK ACROSS THE WAY AND THE same 4 youths were there - PLUS 2 MORE! 'Blessed is he who waits...' (Daniel 12). This is true in evangelism - sometimes we need to wait, and Abba actually INCREASES our harvest! Another example of MISSING and MERCY. We were once in Washington D.C. to tear down spiritual strongholds while Obama was in office and the Holy Spirit

said to us that we needed to listen to a prophetess - like Huldah from the Old Testament 2Ki 22:14 "So Hilkiah the priest, Ahikam, Achbor, Shaphan, and Asaiah went to Huldah the

17

prophetess, the wife of Shallum the son of Tikvah, the son of Harhas, keeper of the wardrobe. (She dwelt in Jerusalem in the Second Quarter.) And they spoke with her." I saw that we had to use 3-way calling on the cellphone and though there were miscommunications, I felt as though Father still showed us great mercy. He had spoken to us that we needed to follow the leadership of the Holy Spirit through this prophetic woman. We saw through prophetic word we had not come up with the right number of laborers - so our mission did not produce as much fruit. So - we resorted to cellphone calls! People with us in Spirit (though not physically with us). Abba really is very merciful! He knows about human limitation and often gives exhortation knowing that we need His mercy to perform what He tells us to do!!!

Many times יְהוָה צְבָא וֹת will give an exhortation, maybe through a dream or vision, that is something you personally have no way of fulfilling. This is true about poor people, many of whom יְהוָה צְבָא וֹת chooses as TRUE prophets. Example - I once visited Jerusalem and went to a wedding of a Jewish believer. He married a beautiful Finnish girl. I then dreamed that I was clothed in bridegroom garments, on an airplane with his Finnish mother-in-law looking down from heaven over Finland. Being a man of meager resources, I wondered

how this could EVER happen. Would you believe, I became friends with a Finnish girl myself in Jerusalem, who I married 2 years later IN JERUSALEM! The Holy Spirit directed me to teach by the gate of the temple, and a troop of Korean prophets were singing and prophesying around the wall. Anni and I had just married, and these Korean prophets walked RIGHT up to

18

Anni, handed her an envelope with 300 dollars plus some shekels in it! This was the DAY AFTER she, in FAITH, bought me a plane ticket to go to Finland so we could

also have a Finnish wedding (to honor her nation and give her poor family members a chance to see us be married). So what began as prophetic dream ended as ? יְהוָה צְבָא וֹת supplying grace upon grace for us to enjoy the blessing of marriage! So do not put anything past צְבָא וֹת יְהוָה

ALL THINGS ARE POSSIBLE WITH HIM!

Prophecy and casting out demons. As I wrote before, the gifts of the Holy Spirit work together. There are many people in the body of Christ all around the earth, and if everything Yahshua יֵשׁוּעַ (Jesus Christ of Nazareth) did were written, there is possibly not enough paper in the entire world to write all the books (see John 21). The gifts of the Spirit, when operating in love and with a body of Christ edifying itself in love, have a snowball effect! Paul exhorted Timothy:

1Ti 4:14Do not neglect the gift that is in you, that was given to you by prophecy with the laying on of the hands of the eldership.

2Ti 1:6Therefore I remind you to stir up the gift of אֱלֹהִים that is in you through the laying on of my hands.

So, we have to STIR up the gifts. Think of cooking. The Holy Spirit is like eggs that are not useful to enrich our foods until we crack open the egg, and stir it. We are like those hard egg shells. Until we are BROKEN, we are not useful to Him. But once we are, out comes the richness of His Spirit. And it forms

19

a rich cake or some other nourishing food to feed the multitudes!

I have been trained by the Holy Spirit to cast out demons. He used people in the body of Christ, who I am very thankful for. They really poured into me and discipled me in these areas. First, if you are binding a spirit, it is important that you do not try to cast it out if the person who is in bondage to it is not ready to repent. Prostitutes often want deliverance, and their minds are in torment, but if they love their wickedness and perversion, casting out the devil will only result in a MORE bound up person filled with 7-fold worse devils! Remember Mary Magdalene?

A prostitute once asked for deliverance. She was full of Jezebel, who lodges in the flesh of women who are fornicating and worshipping idols. She must be confronted and cast out, and she often uses the mouth of her captives against their will. She can fully take over the will of a woman, if they are not indwelt by the Spirit of the LORD. This prostitute was having sharp pain in her side, and I confronted her sin, commanded the evil spirit to leave, and she then reported that she was healed!

However, she then went out driving her hearse (she literally drove a hearse around the city) and she took one of the deacons, who was himself very poor and had lived homeless for some time. She had him trapped and they both left the church. So, clearly, this woman was opening doors for the demons to return with 7-fold strength.

A woman also once came to me in a time of affliction. She seemed distressed by the fact that her daughter was demon-possessed. The Holy Spirit led me to fast and agree in prayer with this lady for the deliverance of her daughter. I went to her house and He directed me to take out bread and grape juice for communion. As soon as I started talking about the blood, the demons fully overtook this young daughter! Her name was Rachel, and the demons had overtaken her body and were causing her to shriek like some wild animal. She also had superhuman strength and her mother and I had to use anointing oil and literally pin her to the ground...as we did, her demons fully manifested - 'I AM SATAN!! I AM SATAN!!' After a very intense battle, and commanding the demons to leave, we finally were talking again to Rachel. She was broken and began to weep and prayed to be BORN AGAIN! She took her first communion right there in the living room and wow did she drink DEEP. O how thankful I am for the blood of the precious LAMB...

Also coming to mind is the time I was ministering among Philippinos overseas. A rabbi and I had visited one of their home churches, and were very blessed and refreshed by the movement of the Spirit in that place! However, 2 people needed deliverance and ONE was the pastor's wife! How embarrassing to have your head pastor's wife need deliverance...but often demons attack the weaker vessel (I think about 70% of the people I personally have seen delivered from demons have been women and children). I have heard other reports of demonic activity from the mission field. But I kid you not, it was like this woman started levitating! Her eyes rolled in her head and looked right at me and the demons screamed profanities.

This same congregation had a young man come in, and his deliverance took about 7 men holding him down. The demons kept saying 'He's mine!!!' Also recently in Finland a number of surprising things happened. One involved a drunk man kicking security guards and me (demons can more easily manifest in people who are drunk) at a Christian conference, but we just looked past the outward manifestation and into the soul of this man and commanded the spirits out!

If you think of people who are demon-possessed as little children who are a slave to some cruel tyrannical slavedriver, then you can really learn to love people and hate the demons operating in them. The lake of fire was made for the devil and his angels according to the Bible so there is nothing wrong with telling demons and Satan that you hate them! Read Psalm 139 - Do I not hate them, O יְהוָה, who hate You? And do I not loathe those who rise up against You?

Psa 139:22I hate them with perfect hatred; I count them my enemies.

Psa 139:23Search me, O אֵל, and know my heart; Try me, and know my anxieties;

Psa 139:24And see if [there is any] wicked way in me, And lead me in the way everlasting.

In fact, the woman whose anointing for casting out devils I have received, would often, after dividing soul from spirit by the WORD to discern and cast out the devils, would say, 'I am

NOT TALKING TO _____ I am talking to the demons. I HATE YOU.' Quite dramatic, but when you could see the people delivered by her ministry and the power of the Holy Spirit operating in her, wow, it was awesome!

I once had a prophetic vision of a Gypsy man. Rev 10:11 And he said to me, "You must prophesy again about many peoples, nations, tongues, and kings."

Gypsies are often prone to violence, stealing and drugs. BUT ABBA LOVES THEM AND SO DO I! He even gave me grace to baptize a Gypsy woman who recently had a baby (they also do not really practice marriage). Pray for the Gypsies!

At any rate, I was under a great time of persecution and had to suffer in the cold (freezing cold). I desperately jumped into a van of a Gypsy family who I had met at church trying to get out of the cold. (They would come for free food.) BUT OUT OF ALL OF THIS, I met a new friend. When they found me in their van, praying in the Spirit, I thought I was dead for sure. (The Gypsies and really anyone, who is on drugs can do something like murder someone when they would never otherwise do something like that.)

Somehow, in spite of the language barrier, I managed to escape from the freezing cold and even though it was awkward, after some time of coffee and Bible study, WE WERE LAUGHING ABOUT THE WHOLE THING! (We had just done something prophetic as a witness against one of the churches in Finland and were suffering great persecution at the hands of the Jezebel spirit and ended up homeless for that night.)

Through it, I befriended a Gypsy man from Sweden. He was bilingual, and helped me talk to the other gypsies, explaining the whole thing. They actually agreed with what we did and were also infuriated by the church system in Finland and a specific pastor who was ravaging the flock in his ravenous greed. At any rate, through all of the chaos, suffering, and fear, out of it came a NEW FRIEND of the Bridegroom. As I wept and poured out my heart, this brother also shared with me his bitterness towards God because if אֵל is so good, why did he allow his daughter to suffer a birth defect?

That night was spent, in a very dangerous place. A young Gypsy came into the room I was trying to sleep in with some kind of crack pipe or something...exhausted and worn out, I managed to sleep a few hours, and get a ride the next day to where I needed to go to get away from the city...Luk 11:49"Therefore the wisdom of אֵל also said, 'I will send them prophets and apostles, and [some] of them they will kill and persecute,'

Abba ultimately delivered us back to my parents' house in America! (He really does great deliverance.) Psa 18:50Great deliverance He gives to His king, And shows mercy to His anointed, To David and his descendants forevermore.

There, I was in my prayer closet, and I saw a vision (prophetic) of this Gypsy man (my friend who was bitter). In the vision (I do not fully understand it), he jumped onto a bus, and his eyes went to a demonic green color (like the color of the pale green

24

horse in Revelation 6 whose rider is DEATH and Hades follows close behind) and then he BEAT SOMEONE VERY BADLY on the bus. So it must have been some kind of spirit of violence.

Many visions are just for the purpose of prayer and intercession. Remember,

If the person under the control of an evil spirit is not ready to repent, BIND the demon. Binding means that you are not permitting the demon to operate.

If they are ready to repent, take communion if possible, get sins confessed and covered by the blood, and then take authority over whatever the spirit is and CAST IT OUT! Send it to Yahshua יֵשׁוּעַ for its instructions.

So, can you see, how the discerning of spirits works with the gift of prophecy to advance Abba's kingdom on earth as it is in heaven in whatever place you are??

Defending the Holy Spirit. Yahshua יֵשׁוּעַ said, 'Mar 8:38 "For whoever is ashamed of Me and My words in this adulterous and sinful generation, of him the Son of Man also will be ashamed when He comes in the glory of His Father with the holy angels' (Mark 8).

We must lay aside the fear of man and choose to be defenders of the Holy Spirit. I remember years ago when I was leading worship at a local homeless shelter. Late in prayer the night before, Abba had revealed to me a song to sing for the next day. When the Bible study leader was touched by the anointing on the worship, he asked 'Where did you get that song from?'

A little embarrassed (for some reason - probably because the church was not so open to the gifts of the Holy Spirit as many churches in America are not), I said, 'That came from the Holy Spirit.' He kind of dismissed me and was not too excited about what I said.

It is very grieving how little of a focus many churches and ministries have placed on the Holy Spirit! It is like they do not acknowledge His lordship as much as they do that of the FATHER and the SON. But much to my discouragement, I have seen that many times we have to defend the Holy Spirit!

Did you receive the Holy Spirit when you believed? This was a question that Paul the apostle asked some believers in Ephesus. Act 19:6 And when Paul had laid hands on them, the Holy Spirit came upon them, and they spoke with tongues and prophesied. Recently in our prayer room in Finland,

I received a vision of a young woman with braided hair. The hair was wrapped around her head, and I first saw part of its fulfillment when we were at a gas station (the cashier had hair like this - I gave her a gospel tract.) Anni and I were later at a rock concert with a group of young evangelist laborers, and we found a young Finnish woman, with braided hair, who was needing to receive the baptism of the Holy Spirit! Anni and I laid hands on her, praying for this blessing to come on her. David Pawson pointed out that one of the signs that you have received the baptism of the Holy Spirit is TRIALS (more so than manifestations like tongues or prophesying). And wow isn't that the truth! I remember when I was first born again, I had such a hunger for church attendance. It was like churches were my new obsession. I remember driving in a car with my mother, around the age of 20, and whereas before

I would notice sinful things (like billboards of adult bookstores), I now had a SHIFT in my focus....churches! I pointed out the window like a little baby and would drive by the churches just looking at them. However, being raised Baptist, we were not so open to the Holy Spirit. Baptists are good at getting people 'saved,'

but when it comes to the deeper things of Yah they tend to try to quiet you down. I pointed to a 'charismatic' church and my mother said, kind of with anger, 'They speak in tongues at that church,' as if to warn me to stay away. Like any child, I gravitated to what my parent said NOT to do! What I found, was a mixture of truth in her warning with error. I found out that when she was born again, the minister strictly forbid my parents to attend churches that operate in the gifts of the Spirit! But as I probed into the realm of charismatic ministry, I was also disgusted with some of the prophetic excess. I understand why Paul gave boundaries and clear commands on HOW to operate in the gifts of the Spirit.

Picture the Holy Spirit as a silent friend who is with you everywhere you go. Even if you go into a place that is mostly wicked, He is with you. People who are against the gospel are going to NOT LIKE this friend, because And when He has come, He will convict the world of sin, and of righteousness, and of judgment:

John 16:9 "of sin, because they do not believe in Me;

John 16:10 "of righteousness, because I go to My Father and you see Me no more;

John 16:11 "of judgment, because the ruler of this world is judged.   John 16:12 "I still have many things to say to you, but you cannot bear [them] now.

 John 16:13 "However, when He, the Spirit of truth, has come, He will guide you into all truth; for He will not speak on His own [authority], but whatever He hears He will speak; and He will tell you things to come.   John 16:14 "He will glorify Me, for He will take of what is Mine and declare [it] to you.

This is true also with churches! Did you know, His Presence has departed from many churches? The Holy Spirit eventually will quietly gather up His - Her things, and quietly leave. I just read how Samson, one of the judges of Israel, did not know יְהוָה אֲדֹנָי had departed from him. He had grieved the Spirit

by revealing the secret of his strength to his Philistine wife, and the strength or power of the Spirit stopped working in him. Could this be a picture of the Jezebel spirit in the last days coveting the anointing of godly men and doing anything she can to take away the strength and power of true men of faith? And church leaders?

I was enamored by this new friend I had made, but also was quickly vaulted into a position of leadership in Campus Crusade for Christ, in my University shortly after my mother and sister led me to Christ through a youth group in Ohio. BOTH our church and Campus Crusade can be very HUSH HUSH about the Spirit. Our church

went so far as to label speaking in tongues as demonic! HOW SAD!! But my friend, David, who was also attending the same university, was baptized with the Spirit. I became his secretive friend. I would pray with him, and was very refreshed by his prayers. BUT I DID NOT WANT CCC TO KNOW ABOUT THIS! I once invited him

to one of our morning prayers meetings (that were very DRY by the way), and David began to speak in tongues! I was a little embarrassed and maybe a little angry (I was waiting at least for an interpretation), and was of course confronted by a woman in the prayer group that this was TOTALLY INAPPROPRIATE. He needed to keep it to himself....was her point. BUT I WAS JUST TRYING TO KEEP UNITY IN OUR SMALL CHRISTIAN GROUP. It became quite a battle in my own mind and soul, one that I still battle to this day. Did I mention, upon finding out that when one of the wives of the pastor of a Russian church we supported (the church I was born again through)

received the baptism of the Spirit, ALL FUNDING WAS CUT TO THIS VERY POOR PASTOR! These are battles that we wrestle with יְהוָֹה אֲדֹנָֽי AND man over...like what is more important - being right or preserving unity in the body of Christ?

How to work around people who are not open to the movement of the Spirit - in prophetic gifting and words of knowledge, etc.

1- Understand that people are all at different levels of maturity in their walk. I view tongues and prophecy as icing on the cake, or dessert in general. If someone is born again, has repented of their sins and received Yahshua יֵשׁוּעַ , they have the MAIN COURSE. They have the CAKE, but NO ICING. They ARE missing out on blessings

and deceived, but they do know יְהוָה אֲדֹנָי DO NOT FORCE people this can actually push them away.

2- Show respect to elders. Women, to your husbands. If you have been filled and tasted the heavenly gift, do not start preaching to an authority figure about how they need to repent for not receiving the baptism of the Holy Spirit. Preaching by women and children is almost always perceived as DISRESPECTFUL and being bossy.

I have noticed a high divorce rate among Pentecostal women specifically. They do not seem to understand how irritating it is to their husbands when their wives preach to them. 1Pe 3:1 Wives, likewise, [be] submissive to your own husbands, that even if some do not obey the word, they, without a word, may be won by the conduct of their wives...

3- If I have received a vision or a dream about someone who I know is Baptist, or not open to the gifts of the Spirit, I often give the word to them in a roundabout kind of way. Instead of saying, 'THE HOLY SPIRIT PROPHESIED TO ME ....' I may say something like, 'YOU KNOW, יְהוָה אֲדֹנָי PUT IT ON MY HEART TO TELL YOU...'

There are ways to give the WORD to someone in a way that will not offend them or their religious preference.

4- Much of it boils down to - DO YOU FEAR יְהוָה אֲדֹנָי Because many believers (especially in America) do not seem to understand that יְהוָה אֲדֹנָי is to be feared. I personally HATE grieving the Spirit, because it decreases FATHER'S Presence in my life, marriage, business dealings and ministry. I HATE IT!!! The Holy Spirit

is a gentleman, who will eventually STOP speaking if we refuse to follow His gentle promptings. Every letter to all 7 churches in Revelation says, 'Rev 2:29 "He who has an ear, let him hear what the Spirit says to the churches."

If you are not listening to the Holy Spirit, you are not REALLY a church.

5- Sad that in the last days, church leadership is corrupt and grieving the Spirit. We have to WORK AROUND their rebellion many times. Read Bible stories about warriors like Gideon and Samson, and how they moved with FAITH. In the last days, Yahshua יֵשׁוּעַ wonders 'Will the Son of Man find FAITH on the earth?' (Luke 18).

Mat 23:13 "But woe to you, scribes and Pharisees, hypocrites! For you shut up the kingdom of heaven against men; for you neither go in [yourselves], nor do you allow those who are entering to go in.' What was true of the religious hypocritical unbelieving Jews in the days of Yahshua יֵשׁוּעַ is true of them now and is also true of many

church people. Living by faith offends compromising harlot churches that are controlled by money, tax-exempt status and other things that grieve the Spirit of יְהוָה אֲדֹנָי and cause religious compromise.

6- Pray for good timing. Of the few times I prophesied to my dad, and he actually received it, TIMING was key. Again, ask the Holy Spirit to help you not cross authority and respect boundaries while at the same time confronting something that you do not agree with. Wives, if your husbands are bound up in foolishness and you need to confront him, REALLY PRAY. Even fast and pray. Do not fight using the flesh. I know many spiritual women who in an attempt to make their husbands more spiritual, have actually resorted to witchcraft (trying to control someone whose authority you are UNDER)

to do it. Jeremiah wrote, 'Cursed is the one who does the work of יְהוָה deceitfully.' Strange to think, but it IS possible. I tried to force my dad to pray with me many times. IF your dad, husband, mother or some other authority figure is too controlling, your response to their control is NEVER to be trying to control them back. That is not your place.

So much Scripture about submission! Wives to husbands, children to parents, younger to elders. SUBMIT YOURSELVES TO אֱלֹהִים resist the devil and he will flee from you (James).

Recently, around Friday the 13th (a high day of witchcraft), I received a dream about a vampire that masqueraded as another believer. This is known as a familiar spirit. I asked the believer if there was ever a consumption of blood in their life. There was, and so

I began to shout at the unclean spirit that got in through drinking blood. It left with a violent shake! Shouting is very important, because demons HATE it when we get bold against the kingdom of darkness. THEY FEAR US. They know that greater is He who is in us than he that is in the world.

Shifting spiritual atmospheres. My wife and I were recently in Latvia on a flight layover on our way to Israel. I had my gospel tract in Latvian printed out and was excited and ready to witness! (What else can you do in an 11 - hour layover??) BUT, thanks be to Father, I first saw that we needed to pray and plow up the ground. Prayer is like water that softens hard clay. SO important to pray in places where evil is rampant so that you do not rebel against Jeremiah's exhortation

For thus says יְהֹוָה to the men of Judah and Jerusalem: "Break up your fallow ground, And do not sow among thorns.

Jer 4:4Circumcise yourselves to יְהֹוָה, And take away the foreskins of your hearts, You men of Judah and inhabitants of Jerusalem, Lest My fury come forth like fire, And burn so that no one can quench [it], Because of the evil of your doings."

Sowing you seed among thorns is unwise in the natural AND the spiritual! Remember what the pigs do when we cast our pearls to them? So, we began to pray and walk around. We noticed some Satanic opposition, and that the enemy was using the authorities at that airport to afflict us. I went up to 3 security guards and started sharing the gospel with them...Anni said she could see the spiritual atmosphere SHIFT in that place! Very powerful!

When we bind and cast out demons and pray and prophesy in places, we are SHIFTING the spiritual atmosphere. Do not underestimate the power of His Spirit working within you!

This also happened in Jerusalem on the Sabbath, when Abba opened a VERY POWERFUL door for us to baptize 2 young men! And that place is a dangerous place to do something like that outside, because it can EASILY attract very NEGATIVE ATTENTION. I was prayer walking in the city, and found a congregation of believers. I AM STILL TRYING TO PROCESS WITH MY FEEBLE MIND EXACTLY WHAT HAPPENED, but all I can write is that when I found Ken, an elder from my past who basically adopted me when I was young in the LORD and was in the wilderness praying and fasting a little too much, in Jerusalem, we were wanting to update each other in the prophetic. (When you get two prophetic people together it is like WATCH OUT!!!) The power of the Spirit fell on the park, and I was talking like a mile a minute because I was so blessed. Suddenly, as I was prophesying or talking and whatever, Ken said something about gatekeepers, and something shifted in the spiritual atmosphere. And then - his cell phone rang... I was speechless (a very rare occurrence.) I knew that something was happening in holiness that my mouth could have caused me to miss. I felt a profound sense of holiness and that my words could grieve the Spirit (have you ever felt that way?)

Isa 43:19Behold, I will do a new thing, Now it shall spring forth; Shall you not know it? I will even make a road in the wilderness [And] rivers in the desert.

1Ki 19:12and after the earthquake a fire, [but] יְהוָה [was] not in the fire; and after the fire a still small voice

Ecc 5:6Do not let your mouth cause your flesh to sin

Did you know the word for 'sin' means to miss the mark? It is an archery term...meaning you MISSED! Sometimes we MISS His voice in a place, because we are too busy, distracted or because the enemy roaring like a lion has put us into the fear of man (or woman, or children or demons or angels). These are sins...and my personal struggle is talking too much, when it is time to be listening! But, blessed be His name, despite the spiritual warfare around Jerusalem, we still managed to do a prophetic dance in the park on the Sabbath to honor Yahshua יֵשׁוּעַ , and the conversation that sparked out of it led to the quick water baptism of these 2 young men! I was humbled and overjoyed to be chosen to have this honor of baptizing these brothers!

Intercessors MUST spread out ... just like evangelists. In fact, my joke for a while has been that Christians are like cow manure, when they are together too much, they STINK! But when you spread manure out, it fertilizes and causes better crop harvest! I am an evangelist. The problem is that if I am co-laboring with another evangelist who is my buddy, sometimes we just talk to each other and we do not effectively reach the Christless multitude standing before us. The same is true with intercessors. When you need to pray or intercede for an upcoming election or a physician who is operating on the sick, DO IT! DO YOUR JOB!!! Or even our prayer lines (by the way, please Skype us for prayer...michaeljanni.j.rhoads) or call 71-GOD-10264 in America - if we just talk ABOUT praying or WHAT we are going to pray about, but do not actually go to the throne of grace, we are in DANGER of SIN).

Reminder - we are called to be SALT and LIGHT! We are called to reach the uttermost parts of the earth with the gospel. The law of Moses is for the rebellious and insubordinate, the murderers of fathers and mothers, and the arrogant. If we only congregate with the righteous and we are always with only other believers, it is possible we are becoming modern-day Pharisees! YUCK! I have seen those tendencies rising up in myself (the religious spirit - one of the most deceptive) and I despise it! TAKE IT OUT OF ME FATHER! MAKE ME HUMBLE AND FILLED WITH LOVE AND WILLING TO EAT WITH THE HARLOTS AND TAX COLLECTORS LIKE YOUR SON DID - EVEN IF RELIGIOUS PEOPLE DESPISE US FOR DOING IT!

So, hey, why don't you ask Abba to break you, to give you a mission field, even if it is just the inner city of your own hometown? Where prostitutes and injustice and wickedness is prevailing? Ask Him to help you HATE demons and the spiritual hosts of wickedness in heavenly places, but to LOVE the people who are bound in chains of injustice and demonic oppression?

False prophets and sex abuse. Many false prophets use sexual forms of control upon those whom they ravage. This is unfortunate, but true. They can be some of the most vicious and deceptive ones out there. This was probably true of the Charles Manson cult (if I remember correctly from a video I saw on them a long time ago). People are often trapped by these false prophets, and made to believe lies, and the fruit of these 'prophets' is often people who resort to suicide, denial of Eloheem אֱלֹהִים (God) or some other extreme behavior.

Years ago, when I was young and impressionable, I began to be interested in the gift of prophecy. I jumped into some ministries that were flowing in the gifts of the Holy Spirit, or so I thought. Having been warned about 'charismatics' by my parents and others, I was naturally curious. I thought, 'What is wrong with speaking in tongues? The Bible talks about it.' I visited inner city Canton, Ohio, where the excitement of drug busts and other kinds of inner city crime kept us in constant prayer and fasting. Songs written by Keith Green kept me fired up to keep reaching these kinds of people! However, one time, a 'prophet' came to the soup kitchen where we were volunteering, that has now become a homeless shelter! People seemed to flock to this man, a handsome African-American male, around 30 years old at the time. The first time I met him, he spoke a word of knowledge that was RIGHT ON. I was very impressed by this man, OUTWARDLY. However, as time went on, some red flags went off. I was at a New Year's celebration, where I found myself losing self-control (I was trying to fast and rarely break them before the plan to do so) I also noticed he had this mind-control or seemingly powerful way of keeping all his disciples focused on himself. A brother opened up to him about a homosexual struggle, and his counsel was that he find a Christian and act out on these desires, reasoning that Jesus had to call demons to the surface before He could cast them out! Excuse me?! Having knowledge about this, I tried to bring him before other spiritual authorities in that city. However, he seemed to always know how to snake his way out of almost any confrontation! I once overheard him preaching and his disciples seemed almost like zombies – it was as though a bomb could have exploded and they would not have even noticed – they were so bedazzled by his prophesying. AH!

Not knowing what to do, I went into the wilderness. I actually spent 10 days in the wilderness, because I was so torn and broken. I knew this was a MAJOR battle, and only about 2 years old in Christ, I was up against a MAJOR Goliath. He was even taking a friend of mine on a 'mission trip' to the Dominican Republic! AH! These kinds of sexual perversions can really warp the minds of both the false prophets and the people they influence. The Bible talks about this - Rom 1:27 Likewise also the men, leaving the natural use of the woman, burned in their lust for one another, men with men committing what is shameful, and receiving in themselves the penalty of their error that was due. I was in the wilderness, and would you believe – אֱלֹהִים gave him justice! It was as though Yahshua יֵשׁוּעַ 's words came to pass – 'Will not אֱלֹהִים avenge His chosen ones who cry out to Him day and night?' (Luke 18). אֱלֹהִים sent me a messenger in the wilderness that this false prophet was now in jail for child molestation! WHEW! The youth told me some of the fruits of this 'prophet.' He said that his friend was once on fire for אֱלֹהִים and was walking in His righteousness. After being 'discipled' by this man, he now hates אֱלֹהִים and wants nothing to do with church. He has forsaken the faith!

So, people who lead cults that have strange and bizarre sexual behaviors are false prophets. I was once ministering among

38

the homeless in southern CA. I was initially blessed by a family who travelled around, feeding the poor, and seemed to have somewhat of a following. We considered joining – possibly doing outreach with them! However, as we examined each other, I was mocked for believing that you need to be married to have sex! They seemed to adopt some kind of spiritual marriage doctrine that I have heard also about in inner city Canton – that people are married by אֱלֹהִים and so do not need to have an actual wedding involving family, courts. What I see this doctrine as is a compromised way of covering over a sin of fornication! Jeremiah prophesied about this kind of covering over sin - <u>Jer 2:35</u> Yet you say, 'Because I am innocent, Surely His anger shall turn from me.' Behold, I will plead My case against you, Because you say, 'I have not sinned.' It is one thing to sin by fornication – it is then another to then DENY that it was sin. I TRY my best, when I am confronted by a prophetic person, if I have sinned, to go by 1 John 2 - <u>1Jo 2:1</u> My little children, these things I write to you, so that you may not sin. And if anyone sins, we have an Advocate with the Father, Yahshua יֵשׁוּעַ Ha Maschiach the righteous. I try to repent quickly! Sexual sin is one of the most deceptive kinds of sin out there! And people wrapped up in it are often self-deceived and deceiving others!

Prophecy and prayer. I have also heard of prophecy coming through extended times of prayer. I once was in prayer and began to see a vision. I saw a friend of mine from Hawai'i driving his car. It was a stick shift. I was praying in the Spirit for a while and the vision started with me seeing a vision of the GRINCH (like the GRINCH WHO STOLE CHRISTMAS) on the top of his stick shift. I quickly realized he was being directed by a deceiving spirit (1 Timothy 4) and needed to tell my friend to get some bad ideas out of his head that the enemy had placed. But this vision came to me during a time of extended prayer.

When and how does prophecy come? And so we have the prophetic word <u>confirmed</u>, that you do well to heed as a light that shines in a dark place, until the day dawns and the morning star rises in your hearts;

<blockquote>

2Pe
1:20
knowing this first, that no prophecy of Scripture is of any private interpretation,

2Pe
1:21
for prophecy never came by the will of man, but holy men of God spoke [as they were] moved by the Holy Spirit.

</blockquote>

Peter one of the beloved apostles of Yahshua יֵשׁוּעַ wrote this. In other words, many people who received prophetic words did not even know what it meant when they received it! Of this salvation the prophets have inquired and searched carefully, who prophesied of the grace [that would come] to you,

<blockquote>

1Pe
1:11
searching what, or what manner of time, the Spirit of Christ who was in them was indicating when He testified beforehand the sufferings of Christ and the glories that would follow.

</blockquote>

The gift of prophecy is one that must be STIRRED up, but my experience has been also that He may fall on me to speak something when I least expect it! The Holy Spirit has all rights to interrupt boring Bible studies and I would say, even church services! I was once in Finland just sitting with a pastor and my wife, when the Holy Spirit began to prophesy

40

through me as we were eating sweet bread and drinking coffee! I had received a dream about this pastor running out of his home, with a frantic look on his face. Little did I know that this man was going to go through the trial of his home burning to the ground! As much as I adored this pastor, I later was distressed to see that his home burning was prophesied as a judgment to a thief to Zechariah the prophet! Then he said to me, "This [is] the curse that goes out over the face of the whole earth: 'Every thief shall be expelled,' according [to] this side of [the scroll]; and, 'Every perjurer shall be expelled,' according [to] that side of it."

> **<u>Zec 5:4</u>**   "I will send out [the curse]," says יְהֹוָה צְבָא וֹת "It shall enter the house of the thief And the house of the one who swears falsely by My name. It shall remain in the midst of his house And consume it, with its timber and stones."

We often do not know what is on the other side of a prophetic word, be it a dream, vision or spoken communication by the Holy Spirit.

What I have found is that it is often:

> 1. Blessings to the obedient

> 2. Curses to the disobedient - For example, I once received a vision of a woman and I was wearing a crown while sitting next to her. Yahshua יֵשׁוּעַ said,

<u>Rev 3:11</u> "Behold, I am coming quickly! Hold fast what you have, that no one may take your crown."

3. By this vision, I knew that my crown, whatever it was that I had labored for, was in danger. And somehow this woman could either MAKE or BREAK my crown. Much of the outcome of this dream hinged on MY OBEDIENCE. Was I going to suffer long at the hands of her husband (my boss), or give in to the fleshly desire to quit my job because it was difficult?

In conclusion, prophecy is like a 2-edged sword. His WORD cuts on the way in, just as much as it does on the way out. If we choose to sow and please the Holy Spirit, we will enjoy the blessing and the crown. If we go the way of our sinful flesh, when our judgment and destruction comes, we cannot complain, because He did warn us! And sometimes 2 or 3 times!

In defense of the sexually abused. Our ministry, Naphtali Services, exists and was birthed by the Holy Spirit to help the gender-confused and sex-abused. We have to see both sides of sexual abuse. While it is true that many people who have been sexually abused often turn around and repeat these same offenses towards others, it is also true that the BLOOD of the Lamb has the power to overcome and destroy these curses (really, this is the ONLY way to overcome- truly)! I was personally molested by my art teacher in 3rd grade, and this behavior went unchecked as I remained in a prison of fear and abuse. I believe I and others who have endured this torment and overcome it by the blood of Messiah and by being born again in the Holy Spirit are in a unique position to help others. 'Blessed be the לֹ הֵים and Father of our Lord Yahshua יֵשׁוּעַ the Messiah, the Father of mercies and אֱל ֹהים of all comfort, <u>2Cr 1:4</u> who comforts us in all our tribulation, that we may be able to comfort those who are in any trouble, with the comfort wherewith we ourselves are comforted by אֱל ֹהים.' AMEN! So we have an ability to comfort others! People who have been abused sexually often have problems with authority. Since it is so difficult to trust authority, there can be a tendency to reject authority all together, speaking of it as evil. Speaking of false prophets, Jude wrote <u>Jud 1:8</u> 'Likewise also these dreamers defile the flesh, **reject authority,** and speak evil of dignitaries.' I noticed personally a tendency in my own spiritual walk to reject spiritual (and other) authorities and speak evil of them, in my younger days in Christ. Perhaps the encounter with this false prophet mixed with the 3rd grade incident gave me this view. I had to really see the roots of my tendencies to revile pastors and male leaders as the Holy Spirit revealed them. Then, ask אֱל ֹהים to uproot these tendencies in me. ' אֱל ֹהים please expose my own tendencies to speak evil of others, and remove them from me. By the blood of Your precious Son, I claim His resurrection power and victory to overcome the distrust of authority, and I stand on Your WORD that ALL authority has been given to Your Son in whose name I pray AMEN'

Remember, before you write someone off as a false prophet, understand that they may be coming out of a very abusive experience. They may have spent 10 years under the authority of a sexually abusive husband and are severely wounded. These kinds of people often claim the Holy Spirit tells them things that you may question. Father is gracious, full of mercy and compassion, and slow to anger. Do not be too quick to condemn others as false prophets when they may just be immature, abused or not yet discipled in this gift of the Spirit. Perhaps the Father is calling YOU to take this person under your wing! Be merciful as He is!

Homelessness and false prophecy... Years ago, on my first sabbatical, I was on Oahu. I had spent almost a year raising funds, fasting and praying and communicating with people there before moving in faith to this island. I knew no one before going, save one teammate from my university swimming team. So this was really a step of faith! I found out that there was a lot of homelessness on Oahu, and mental illness. I felt this information was revealed to me as an exhortation from the Holy Spirit to minister to these people!   I would find them sleeping in little communities near parks and would get off from work and go minister to them. In fact, one time the Holy Spirit told me to throw a bottle cap away in a specific dumpster behind a grocery store (sounds like a strange instruction from the Holy Spirit, but read on) after work, and when I did this, I noticed that this store had wastefully thrown away VERY GOOD FOOD! All kinds of unopened granola bars, half-gallons of orange juice, and so on! And down the street was the homeless community, sleeping in their dirty tents...amazing! I went 'dumpster diving' against the wisdom of many people and had a little feeding ministry going on, by the Holy Spirit! BUT, in my interactions with some of these people, I met a woman named GRACE. She was Philippina, and I soon found out that she was the victim of false prophecy! She was sent to Oahu by a supposed 'prophetess,' the fruit of whose prophecies I saw being a precious elderly woman sleeping at a bus stop! It broke my heart! And enraged me all at the same time. True prophets LOVE JUSTICE, because our Father also loves justice (Isa 61:8 "For I, יְהֹוָה, love justice; I hate robbery for burnt offering; I will direct their work in truth, And will make with them an everlasting covenant.") True prophets do not like seeing HOMELESSNESS! They do not like seeing people being treated with less care than what many animals receive in rich peoples' homes! (Do not even get me started on how people pay money for dog food and veterinary visitation and are not willing to pay for a homeless person to sleep in a hotel for a few nights.) So, do you really believe that a true prophet is going to send a disciple to a place to endure those kinds of trials? I guess it is possible, but any good prophet or spiritual mentor is going to be willing to SUFFER WITH (that is what 'compassion' means) those they are sending into jungles or other dangerous places with the gospel. (Note – I do not know WHO was this prophet, and I did not have their side of the story…the Bible does say you need 2 or 3 witnesses to establish a matter, and I only heard what Grace said.)

We encountered the same thing in Washington D.C. My wife and I went there to intercede for the government and visit two brothers from IHOP, and we found ourselves pulled by the Spirit to bless the homeless downtown. As we drove with our food provisions, we jumped out in the cold and ran up to them. One woman, looked out of her blanket and when we asked her how we can pray for her, said, 'Pray that I know what my ministry calling is!' I thought this to be very interesting! Do not get me wrong … I know אֱלֹהִים does call people from all walks of life – rich, poor, farmers, fishers, rabbis, and so on, but I can also see that people are often led astray by false prophecies into trouble and danger. And when

45

the shepherds are like the ones Zechariah prophesied about (WORTHLESS – 'Woe to the worthless shepherd, Who leaves the flock!, Zech. 11), they are often not willing to go and seek out their sheep who have wandered from the fold. Not only do they do this, but they also fulfill what Ezekiel prophesied "The weak you have not strengthened, nor have you healed those who were sick, nor bound up the broken, nor brought back what was driven away, nor sought what was lost; but with force and cruelty you have ruled them.' (Ez. 34) I would say they are the ones driving them away! And once they are driven away, would like to forget about them!

Let's get something straight. The law of Moses declares, Deu 19:15 "One witness shall not rise against a man concerning any iniquity or any sin that he commits; by the mouth of two or three witnesses the matter shall be established." As I was writing this book, I spoke to my wife about some of what I wrote. She said, 'Abba often says things 2 or 3 times if it is truly prophetic.' Confirmation! So, before you go vaulting off to some drug community or try to move into a neighborhood where there is sex slavery, make sure you have heard 2 or 3 exhortations from the Spirit to do so! Then you KNOW it is Him, and not just some notion you have to try and be a hero for the kingdom – in your own flesh. You do not want to end up homeless against His will.

A recent communication we have received 2 or 3 times has been one that is somewhat puzzling to me. The first came as a vision where I saw some kind of balance SWING to California and it had 3 jewels on the scale. Hmmm….then, a few weeks later, while praying with an elderly woman after the Sabbath meeting, I saw ANOTHER vision of scales, that pertained to

Daniel 5 and marriage - "And this is the inscription that was written: MENE, MENE, TEKEL, UPHARSIN.

Dan 5:26 "This is the interpretation of [each] word. MENE: אֱלֹהִים has numbered your kingdom, and finished it;
Dan 5:27 "TEKEL: **You have been weighed in the balances, and found wanting...**

We shared the vision with the woman and another spiritual leader in Finland. The vision: The statue of liberty was holding the scales, and it was WAY off balance because Anni and I were standing on one side, and there was NO ONE on the other side. The leader said this is a prophecy to us that אֱלֹהִים is going to raise up another married couple to help us, or balance us in some way. I believe this prophecy is showing also that AMERICA has been weighed in the scales and found wanting – in the area of marriage. (Shortly after I receive the vision, I read online that Obama did some foolish thing that supports gay marriage.) And then, would you believe, the vision came a THIRD time!? This time, the vision was of a ladder leaning on a tree where I was working helping an elderly man reconstruct his front porch, and I saw a golden scale and it was sliding off the ladder (the ladder was at an angle – not perpendicular to the ground). HMMM...I am still chewing on this, but think of this Scripture - Gen 41:32 "And the dream was repeated to Pharaoh twice because the thing is established by אֱלֹהִים, and אֱלֹהִים will shortly bring it to pass.' So, clearly there is some assignment my wife and I have together that involves BALANCE and we are needing the Holy Spirit to lead us (pray for us) because it probably involves prophesying against gay marriage...in America?

So, going back to the homeless, I can see that many of them legitimately have a prophetic gift! (The Bible says, 'The Son of Man has no place to lay His head.') My wife and I were once forced to sleep on the floor of a Greyhound bus station where I was subsequently KICKED by some kind of security guard around 8 in the morning, partly because the lady we asked to take us in for the night said NO! I tried to explain our situation and she refused to take the least of His brothers and sisters in as strangers (Matthew 25 ring a bell?) So she was acting like a goat, and we suffered as a result. But I believe that is different. Perhaps this woman on Oahu ran out of money and could not afford a return flight to the Philippines. I don't know! One thing for sure – do not run off to some desert island because one person came and gave you a prophecy, without elder covering! Many times a prophet will be sent just to confirm something that Abba has already been nudging you to do. This happened to me one time at an abortion clinic. I wanted to preach, there was even an organized group there with a megaphone (this doctor had crossed many lines, had many lawsuits against him and had done atrocious things like killing even one mother with a mental disability in addition to her unborn child), but just needed a little nudge. A woman came up and said, 'PREACH!' She seemed urgent and her eyes were filled with justice and compassion. That was all I needed to step up and speak against him – but this was something Father had already been pulling on me to do...

GOING OVERBOARD. This is somewhat of a joke, and this is an area where I personally have made error a number of times. This is when we get into performance-based obedience and believe Abba's love is based on our performance. People can develop of spirit of religious perfectionism where they equate righteousness with how well they play their guitar during worship sets, or how good their punctuation is in their missionary prayer letter. THIS IS A LIE! This kind of spirit can also filter into exhortations from the Holy Spirit. I believe that the Holy Spirit DOES lead us to do radical things like sit all night with the homeless and so on, but what happens is that sometimes we go TOO FAR with something. This kind of religious spirit can partner with a spirit of competitive jealousy, and what results is DISASTER – possibly to someone's physical health, or even worse, their spiritual health. 2Cr 10:12 For we dare not class ourselves or compare ourselves with those who commend themselves. But they, measuring themselves by themselves, and comparing themselves among themselves, are not wise. Person A may feel the need to pray for 3 hours, and person B finds out and must then pray for 4 hours. I see that being competitive is not a sin, but in our spiritual life, it can be pushed into that. I had a friend once whom I baptized. He was Mexican. I noticed that he was competitive, and would take him out evangelizing. I would realize that on our bikes it could become a bike race if I was not careful. I had to check myself – we are out here to win souls, not RACE. The most tragic thing was that a few years later I ran into him in Jerusalem, and found out that he had forsaken faith in Christ and was now practicing Judaism! AH! Many prophetic people give exhortations to start keeping commandments from the Old Testament, such as the Sabbath, the dietary laws from the Old Testament, and the Feasts, and I myself have responded to these exhortations! But once I see people begin to dress in black like orthodox Jews and begin worshiping on the Sabbath in orthodox synagogues, I see that the exhortation has been taken TOO FAR. To the point of sin! (It is obviously a sin to forsake Yahshua יֵשׁוּעַ). This can also be true with fasting. We need to make sure we are accountable to elders and members in the body of Christ if we are doing radical prophetic things. With fasting, person A announces that he fasted for 7 days, without eating food and only drinking water. Person B, very competitive, decides he needs to fast for 10 days... Many of these spiritual errors can be corrected if we obey Yahshua יֵשׁוּעַ and just keep these kinds of spiritual disciplines to ourselves like He said (read Matthew 5). Also, consider what Yahshua יֵשׁוּעַ said about prayer - <u>Mat 6:6</u> "But you, when you pray, go into your room, and when you have shut your door, pray to your Father who [is] in the secret [place]; and your Father who sees in secret will reward you openly." Have you ever considered that HOW LONG you pray does not matter as much as the QUALITY of your prayer time? I have felt much more accomplished in the Spirit the times that I have been travailing in prayer, maybe even only for a few minutes, than 30 minutes of vain repetition.

I was guilty of this performance-based spirituality when I was first born again. I had lived my life before Christ as a competitor in almost everything – academics and athletics. A joke in my family was that we even had a competition to see who would brush their teeth the quickest! I realized, through a sister in Christ, that I was making others feel less spiritual around me. She said something like, 'When I am around you, I feel like a horrible Christian!' While it is one thing to bring others to conviction by living a holy life, it is completely another (spiritual pride) to constantly be broadcasting how you stayed up all night praying, or how long you fasted and how much the Holy Spirit always talks only to you, seemingly. In fact, these kinds of 'all eyes on me' prophets often become false prophets. Think of Joseph Smith – the false prophet of the Mormon heresy whose supposed plates given through an angelic visitation have yet to be discovered. He was out over spiritualizing his experiences and eventually decided he was so spiritual that every other church was false and only HE was right. How many Mormons are without the TRUE saving knowledge of Christ because of this man??

Religious spirits. People may accuse you of having a religious spirit, meaning an evil spirit that says spiritual sounding things. These REALLY do exist. Here are some Scriptures - 'The Jews all know the way I have lived since I was a child, from the beginning of my life in my own country, and also in Jerusalem. They have known me for a long time and can testify, if they are willing, that according to the strictest sect of our religion, I lived as a Pharisee. And now it is because of my hope in what Eloheem has promised our fathers that I am on trial today. This is the promise our twelve tribes are hoping to see fulfilled as they earnestly serve Him day and night. O king, it is because of this hope that the Jews are accusing me. Why should any of you consider it incredible that Eloheem raises the dead??' Acts 26. Paul was on trial! If anyone came out of a religious background, it was Paul. And he wrote 13 of the books of the New Testament (Brit Chadashah)! The point I am trying to make is that not all religion is bad. James says that 'Religion that is pure and undefiled in the eyes of the Creator is that we look out for widows and the fatherless and keep ourselves from the pollutions of the world.'

THAT WRITTEN, I can show you also in Scripture that demons say things through people that are sometimes true -

'Just then a man in their synagogue who was possessed by an evil spirit cried out, 'what do you want with us, Jesus of Nazareth? Have you come to destroy us? I know who you are - the Holy One of God!' Mark 1 Notice, those demons are right - he WAS the HOLY ONE OF GOD (and Is and ALWAYS WILL BE!!) I am not sure how demons get their information, but they do seem to know things and blurt things out before the time they are to be spoken. Why do you think Yahshua יֵשׁוּעַ did not permit the demons to speak, because they knew who He was?

A perfect example of a religious spirit that is demonic is the spirit of anorexia. Paul wrote that in the last days, demons would forbid food and biblical marriage (1 Timothy 4). Many young believers become zealous to obey God and get bound up by a religious spirit that ends up deceiving them about the blessings of food and marriage. In zeal to do something radical for the kingdom, people may wander off into the wilderness for a long period of time, and come back looking like a skeleton. THIS IS NOT FROM GOD! Elijah and Moses and other prophets who did those things had supernatural power from the Holy Spirit...plus they are not the one we are to imitate - Yahshua יֵשׁוּעַ is our example. Notice that when Yahshua יֵשׁוּעַ came back from the wilderness, 'He returned to Galilee in the power of the Spirit, ... and He taught in their synagogues...' Luke 4. It does not say that He returned from His wilderness fast, and had to be rushed to the hospital and put onto life support. If you closely read the gospels about His fast, it only says HE ATE NOTHING. he probably had some

52

kind of liquid diet like drinking milk or something. ASK HIM.
.

Another example of a demonic religious spirit is one that was revealed to me in a dream. Allow me to give the exact dream. (help me HOLY SPIRIT!) In the dream, I was given a preaching platform at a major church. I came a long way to give testimonies about overseas mission work. However, when I showed up, the head pastor said 'Oh, you are not allowed to preach anymore...' I realized I was lured by a false promise. I was infuriated that this pastor had supposedly given me a platform to preach, and as he was saying WHY, he said, 'BESIDES, YOUR DAD BELIEVES THE SABBATH IS NOT SUNDAY!!' So, this particular demonic religious spirit spoke something that is true (the Sabbath is NOT Sunday).

Demons actually do say very foolish things and they are usually just irritations to us meant to provoke us to anger. We all must guard our mouths because Satan could use any of our mouths if we are not careful. Remember Peter? A recent demonic manifestation happened at our church in Finland (the one I wrote about earlier). In this church, we WERE given a preaching platform and freedom to lead worship and give testimonies about our ministry in Jerusalem, on a Sunday meeting (NOT THE SABBATH). Right before we got up to testify, a spirit manifested among an elderly widow who volunteers in the church - saying that my wife had to go buy more bread for the meeting. This was an evil spirit using her mouth, but it was just to provoke us to anger (THE TABLE WAS FULL OF BREAD AND WE DID NOT NEED ANY MORE AND THE MEETING WAS STARTING VERY SOON - do you really think ABBA would say something like that?? By the way, there are demons that put you on the 'runaround' to try to keep you rushing and busy and always doing things when you are supposed to be sitting at His feet).

The way I knew it was an evil spirit was because after, when our friend who also was a church elder, came over to fellowship with us after the meeting, I was talking about it, and I STARTED LAUGHING SO HARD THAT TEARS WERE POURING DOWN MY FACE! If you have ever been delivered from an evil spirit, sometimes joy accompanies deliverance and brings a release of your emotions. It is beyond human intellect or understanding.

That's where biblical marriage is very important in the last days. Picture you and your spouse (or future spouse) as young school kids. You have a cruel teacher who controls everything you do. This teacher hawks over you, abuses you, calls you stupid and the classroom is more an environment of fear and more like a prison cell than a place of growth and learning. And on top of that, the teacher is demanding money for this, and teaching you LIES. But at least you have another student in the classroom that you love...that is a picture of the Jezebel and Balaam spirits in the last days operating in churches and schools. Jezebel and Balaam love operating in churches and schools. Jezebel loves sexual immorality and will bless homosexual unions and fornication, but will oppose marriage of the righteous. (She knows her preaching and teaching platform could be removed by people that are ACTUALLY anointed and connected with the Father.) Many disciples of Yahshua יֵשׁוּעַ go to churches, and are abused financially by a money-hungry Balaam spirited pastor, told lies about the Sabbath and forced to worship idols such as CHRISTMAS

TREE and believe lies such as that Christ was born on December 25th. When you have a spouse, you can talk about these things and LAUGH ABOUT THEM later. In fact, Anni and I are learning to laugh in the face of the devil because we are that confident that our Father will ALWAYS deliver us...Babylon (the WORLDWIDE church system that is wrapped up in the Jezebel spirit, reverse headship (women preachers, and men being effeminized) and greed and love of money and even the worldwide abortion epidemic) is a very demonic and yet very powerful force that truly prophetic people have to deal with in the last days. (See Revelation 17 and 18). NOT FUN! But thanks be to Eloheem that we can overcome lies that the 'CHURCH' feeds us and have truly love for our brothers and sisters. Some of the strongest bonds of fellowship I have had with my brothers and sisters in Messiah have been ones formed during times of persecution. It's like 'Hey we are running for our lives but at least we are together!!!'

Balaam vs. Jezebel. Of the 7 churches in Revelation, only 2 of them were NOT told to repent. The spirits of Balaam and Jezebel are like a REALLY BAD MARRIAGE. Both of them are DEMONS that operate IN CHURCHES in the last days and are dealing with sexual immorality and idol worship. There are so many warnings from the apostles about idol worship and sexual immorality! 'Beloved, keep yourselves from idols' (1 John 5). Here are some signs that a religious spirit is operating in your congregation that is covering over sexual immorality.

1 - Pastor seems to live too secretive of a life (possible pornography addiction) - always has to be alone in his office

2 - Witchcraft prayers - when people pray for others to commit adultery so they can get divorces and remarry someone else (sad but this does actually happen)

3- Women dressed very immodest and looking like harlots, and when confronted, they talk back and justify what they are doing

4- Icons to Mary or other saints, crucifixes, prayer rosaries...even cartoon gospel tracts can be idols...

Idolatry is one of the most subtle and yet deadly forces that destroy and weaken churches. I used to resist any and all forms of photography, but I have seen how the Holy Spirit can use photographs, so I am trying not to be so black and white in my thinking. I, however, became obsessed with MY OWN MINISTRY! (an idol) to the point of neglecting other commandments. In fact, I got into a fight with a disciple about using a cell phone to take photographs of what we were doing in Jerusalem...he said I was making idols, I said I was honoring my mother who was unable to make the Jerusalem pilgrimage. What is the truth???

At any rate, idolatry is a root sin that leads to many other bizarre behaviors, including homosexuality (see Romans 1). Question - do you really use all your technology (computers, cell phones ipads, iPods, twitter, face book, Skype on so on) for the kingdom? Are you REALLY crucified with Christ in your usage of these things, or are you SELFISH in the usage of them? There are areas we need to wrestle with Yah in the last days. Yahshua יְשׁוּעַ only did what He saw the Father do....How does Yahshua

יֵשׁוּעַ see His Father using all of this technology in the last days??

Walking contrary to the Jezebel spirit

We recently were in a synagogue, where we gave testimony of Abba's mighty works through us. The pastor preached on the Jezebel spirit, and how this devil seeks to undermine male authority in both the home and churches/synagogues. Having just completed a year serving in Finland, where that spirit operates in probably 7-fold strength, as compared to America, I had ears to hear! I was reflecting on what the anointing taught me over there. Here is the testimony:

A woman in our church had the keys to the church. She had a strong lust spirit and would even talk with leadership about how she was not afraid to commit adultery. Because the church was in a time of tumult with weak leadership, no one did anything about this. I had a few confrontations with her, one being when her daughter came pounding on our door in tears, because her mother had gone psycho. We walked outside of our apartment, and her daughter brought us to the sauna, where her mother was shrieking like an animal. The ambulance came, and in spite of trying to rebuke the unclean spirits, they still took her away to be institutionalized. We were then put in charge of her daughter by the authorities (her father was not in the picture)…

Yahshua יֵשׁוּעַ said, "Indeed I will cast her into a sickbed, and those who commit adultery with her into great tribulation, unless they repent of their deeds.

Rev 2:22

> **Rev 2:23**   "I will kill her children with death, and all
> the churches shall know that I am He who

57

searches the minds and hearts. And I will give to each one of you according to your works.

WE SAW THIS LITERALLY HAPPEN! Although her daughter was not killed, this woman was put on a sickbed. And yet we noticed she was quick to vault herself to the front page of the local newspaper when they came and photographed the work we were doing in food distribution to the poor. After she was released from the hospital, we were VERY cautious about this woman. However, only being deacons, our authority was limited. Knowing however that I have a prophetic gift that I was operating in in that church, I knew I was a target for the Jezebel spirit and her operations within that congregation. (Jezebels attract MORE – the longer you tolerate her in your family and ministry, the MORE that will come and before you know it, you have an INFESTATION of Jezebel.) One day, I left my guitar at the church and needed to go back, and my clothing was pulled on and also the children of Jezebel are as violent and lustful in their desire for power and position – the Gypsy children would resort also to violence against me and יְהוָֹה אֲדֹנָי.

Though I was locked into this position for one year, I knew I needed to war against this spirit. Even a dwarf came in and tried to control the preacher one time (Jezebel manifests through unsuspecting people – often abused, and sick and bitter people)! My wife said she was trying to bind that Jezebel spirit because she was loudly interrupting the preaching...

BUT, through all the suffering, I learned obedience! Just like Yahshua יֵשׁוּעַ . Abba taught me a spiritual warfare tactic in conquering Jezebel – DO THE OPPOSITE OF ALMOST EVERYTHING SHE SAYS. For example, if a Jezebel spirit is trying to control you, and you are working with one in a food ministry, if she comes and barks an order at you, DO THE

58

OPPOSITE. I did this, and literally, the probably 4 or 5 women that would GANG UP on me each week at the food distribution outreach, would eventually give up, get tired, and stop annoying me. It was hilarious! In fact, a few times, when an elder came to see how we were doing, some of the manifestations of the Jezebel spirit through particularly some of the VERY OLD WOMEN would be cause for hilarious laughter as we would tell him about it! We would honestly just laugh off all of her attacks and continue warring against them by WALKING CONTRARY.

Let me give you Scripture to support what I am writing: 'Then, if you walk contrary to Me, and are not willing to obey Me, I will bring on you seven times more plagues, according to your sins.

| **Lev 26:22** | I will also send wild beasts among you, that will rob you of your children, destroy your livestock, and make you few in number; and your highways shall be desolate. |

| **Lev 26:23** | 'And if by these things you are not reformed by Me, but walk contrary to Me, |

| **Lev 26:24** | **then I also will walk contrary to you**, and I will punish you yet seven times for your sins. |

This is Abba speaking to Israel, as He warned them through the prophet Moses. HE IS WARNING US TOO THAT JEZEBEL WALKS CONTRARY TO HIM. She is a wayward wife, a filthy

harlot. She has NO LOVE OF יְהוָה or for the things of His Spirit. She is in your church and family to kill, steal and destroy (I am talking about that spirit – NOT the people she manifests through.) Her prayers are prayers of WITCHCRAFT And she can attack you through men too! Just keep in mind how strong the

homosexual spirit is in the last days. IT IS ALL OVER THE
EARTH, INCLUDING JERUSALEM! She covets your anointing,
and she is planning her attacks. She has organized attacks and in her
abominable lusts, she will even resort to murder if she does not get
her way. So consider yourself warned, and when you notice her

operations in your sphere of influence, just as Abba יְהוָה does, so
must you, WALK CONTRARY TO HER.

Prophesying can be dangerous. ...an intercessor once
asked me in Jerusalem if anyone ever died as a result of
my prayers. ?? Interesting question - somewhat morbid,
but I realized quickly that he wanted to tell me a story
about what happened when he prayed against wickedness
in a place. Prophetic works are very powerful...

Eze
11:13

Now it happened, while I was prophesying, that
Pelatiah the son of Benaiah died. Then I fell on my
face and cried with a loud voice, and said, "Ah,
יְהוָה אֲדֹנָי! Will You make a complete end of the
remnant of Israel?"

Prophesying can actually KILL people! By the sword of
the WORD, we speak life to what is of Him, and death to
what is not. I was once with some intercessors near
Galilee where Yahshua יֵשׁוּעַ Himself was often with His
disciples. I prophesied and found out that around the
time of this prophecy, a death occurred. I felt some kind
of anointing on this word. (Death is not always bad by
the way. Sometimes death can be deliverance to a
suffering person, like a very elderly person in a nursing
home.) The Bible also says, 'Life and death are in the
power of the tongue.' Our words, especially when they

60

are His words, can cut through demonic principalities and hosts of wickedness and truly bring the kingdom on earth as it is in heaven!

I once visited a skateboarding park with a friend on Oahu, Hawai'i. I began to pray and share the gospel. I think because I had been in the wilderness fasting and praying, there was some kind of the fear of יְהוָה אֲדֹנָי upon me. That skateboarding park cleared out quick! My friend commented on what happened. This kind of thing was somewhat of a normal occurrence to me, but was quite shocking to him. Prophecy has the power to calm a storm, and to raise the dead! It is no small thing for our Father יְהוָה אֲדֹנָי to even control the weather as we speak prophetically.

Prophecy in your community. I had noticed some spiritual darkness in our village in Polvijärvi, Finland. Anni could also see we needed to do something prophetic. As we walked and prayed, I took oil and anointed some wood sticks and pushed them into the ground (not sure if this is totally biblical, but the concept of anointing is). We then visited a pregnant Gypsy woman and prayed over her womb and for the unborn child. We were very glad to see her, and she gave us a testimony that she did not become pregnant until she was born again - had been trying for 7 years! When we returned, somehow a spirit of darkness or death had entered our dwelling-place. We had to call to the USA for prayer and then begin to pray against the darkness that had found its way into our place. Many times יְהוָה אֲדֹנָי

sends prophets from one area to another area to do a work, and then get out of there. It is often a quick work, almost like a mission trip. When you live in a community and plan to be there for a while, it is not always wise to try to come against principalities or to do prophetic things. Yahshua יֵשׁוּעַ said, 'A prophet has no honor in his hometown.' My suggestion - if you hunger for prophetic witness, ask יְהוָה אֲדֹנָי to send people to your community who are prophets.

My family once moved to Kansas - and our prophetic assignment was to shut down an abortion clinic. We did our work, and then got out of there! Abba really does like to shield His kids from excessive persecution. I have also seen many times where prophetic assignments were given, and people in my family or community did not really know about it. Prophecy is often a call that one receives, is removed from a community for a season to fulfil, and then is returned to their community. <u>Amo 3:7</u> Surely יְהוָה אֲדֹנָי will do nothing, but he reveals his secret unto his servants the prophets. The Father often calls people as His prophets, the ones whom He can entrust secret information. And we do best to HEED our calling! Think of David – not only was he a king, he was also a prophet! Many of his Psalms were and are prophetic. When David was not obedient to his callings, he fell into sin! So when How about Amos? He was given a call in the middle of his farming career. <u>Amo 7:15</u> Then יְהוָה אֲדֹנָי took me as I followed the flock, And יְהוָה אֲדֹנָי said to me, 'Go, prophesy to My people Israel.' My wife and I were given a call to the people of

Haiti. They were broken and hurting from the earthquake that took the lives of many of their family members – many had come to America (New York) seeking refuge. I am also reminded of a dream that the Father gave me. In the dream, a youth whom I had been called to disciple in the prophetic was visiting his grandparents. I was spending too much time on a garage sale with my parents in their house, and as I doled the time away, I looked across the street (his grandparents were living across the way from my parents' house) to see him being put into a baby chair by his grandparents!

So what I believe יְהוָה אֲדֹנָי is saying is that if you are gifted prophetically, not only are you called to use this give, but you are also called to disciple younger believers. Remember the commission of the Master Yahshua יֵשׁוּעַ Himself - Go therefore and make disciples of all the nations, baptizing them in the name of the Father and of the Son and of the Holy Spirit,

Mat 28:20 "teaching them to observe all things that I have commanded you; and lo, I am with you always, [even] to the end of the age." Amen. His final instruction to us is to replicate Himself! To cause Christ to be formed in others and to develop the gifts placed by the Holy Spirit in us and others. So, when the call comes, RESPOND TO IT! And expect resistance from your family. Maybe even expect to go alone. Many prophets as you read in Scripture are called by themselves, and Father, for whatever reason, singles them out for a specific work. This was true of Jonah, Elijah, and even Yahshua יֵשׁוּעַ . BUT – also I give a word of caution. Prophetic people are sometimes prone to isolating themselves, and thinking that they are all alone.

Remember, when Elijah went into the wilderness to fast and pray? Rom 11:4 But what does the divine response say to him? "I have reserved for Myself seven thousand men who have not bowed the knee to Baal." Sometimes at low points in our prophetic ministry, that is exactly when Abba comes in with His message of comfort! Prophecy is a calling to comfort but remember you reap what you sow – sometimes from the Father Himself!

Watch out for false prophets, many of them are very beautiful!

And no wonder! For Satan himself 2Cr 11:14 transforms himself into an angel of light.

Paul here was warning the church in Corinth about false apostles, but I believe the principle applies to false prophets as well. Earlier, I wrote about a prophetic dream I received where Father sent a group of us to Kansas City to witness the miraculous healing of a young man who had been bound in a wheelchair for months. When we arrived, we found ourselves at the end of a semester (?) of young IHOP students. The genuine revival fire that had fallen was burning in the hearts of these students, and they were like walking Holy Spirit vessels! So refreshing to be around. They would talk about names of 'prophets' who were mostly just worship leaders in their 24/7 prayer room (if you get a chance, check out www.ihop.org/prayerroom). Knowing the Father had sent us, I just jumped right in to a lot of what was going on. VERY DANGEROUS! Any time there is true revival, and accompanying miracles, signs and wonders, we have to be careful because Satan comes to steal, kill and destroy stronger in these kinds of environments than in other places. So, I noticed, among all the name dropping (I would hear, '_____ IS LEADING WORSHIP RIGHT NOW!!!' or 'Did you hear the worship set by _____?') that the focus was shifting from יְהוָה אֱלֹהִים to the people who were singing. (Quite beautifully, I might add.)

Remember, no temptation has overtaken you except what is COMMON to man (1 Corinthians 10:13). Even John the beloved apostle was tempted to worship an angel!

<u>Rev 22:8</u> Now I, John, saw and heard these things. And when I heard and saw, I fell down to worship before the feet of the angel who showed me these things.

The angel rebuked him! So, as I found myself refreshed by the TRUE worship in Spirit and truth, I was also TEMPTED to fall into the worship of the WORSHIP LEADERS. NOT GOOD! Father יְהוָה אֱלֹהִים then gave me a wakeup call when I discovered how blatantly FALSE one of the prophecies of one of the worship leaders was (one of the big names at IHOP). Actually, there were 2 SEVERE red flags about her that I found as I went onto YouTube and listened to some of her 'prophecies.' One was her saying before quite a large audience at a church (1 Cor. 14 says that women are to KEEP SILENT in the church in the context of prophesying) that the next president would have a mantle like Deborah the prophetess and judge of Israel. This was right before OBAMA got into office! Excuse me? I then, was getting more and more grieved by seeing all kinds of gender confusion operating in that ministry (something that our ministry, Naphtali Services, is called to destroy in the church. We were definitely in the right place at the right time, but our assignment was not to 'go

65

with the flow' in this area.) I would hear women, such as women prophesying like they were the BRIDEGROOM and how much she longed for her bride. While I understand that when we prophesy, sometimes there is an utterance that transcends gender barriers in the natural, it can still sow much confusion into the mind of a young believer who may have come out of homosexuality and needs deliverance. The reverse is true as well (men constantly talking about how they are the bride of Christ.)

So, how I responded specifically to this was to speak against it! People began to be angry at me (she was one of the IHOP superstars!!!) and I even found her husband at the prayer altar at one of the services. I confronted him, in love, and suggested that he cover his wife a little better, like maybe ask her to run her prophecies by him before she broadcasts (especially the false ones) before large church audiences that the TRUE APOSTLE Paul said women are NOT SUPPOSED TO DO! I mean, if you are going to disobey the Bible, ladies, you may as well speak something TRUE if you are truly prophetic!!! What I began to do, is, if she was leading worship during a meeting, I would gracefully walk out of the church and go do something else...I refuse to sit under a WOMAN when Paul exhorts us NOT TO, especially when she is speaking false things. BUT HER MUSIC IS SO PRETTY!!!!

Here is an excerpt from our newsletter, where we exposed another false prophet(-ess)... ***Note – I do not have anything against women (I am married to one.)

One of the most powerful prophetic people I know is a woman. Both examples just happen to be women.***
Thanks to Eloheem אֱל הִים (AKA GOD), who gives us the ANOINTING of His Spirit!

> But the anointing that you have received from Him abides in you, and you do not need that anyone teach you; but as the same anointing teaches you concerning all things, and is true, and is not a lie, and just as it has taught you, you will abide in Him.

1Jo 2:27

Here is my version:

Our technology guy, Kenny Samples, was given a preaching platform. We had two prophetic dreams that spoke of our authority in the churches, plus at the American New Year, Abba instructed us to "visit the lampstands." The first dream (received by Kenny) was someone giving him a check for a LARGE amount of money saying, "GO AND GET THAT CHURCH YOU HAVE BEEN WAITING for." Last week, I was pumped to hear that an inner city lady preacher (who ended up being exposed as a Jezebel tonight - it took 7 years for us to figure this out!) was YIELDING her preaching platform to Kenny - or so we thought.

Kenny diligently studied the WORD - in fact, I had to call him because I have been working (secular) tearing down wallpaper and light electrical to make some money for overseas. He was filled with the WORD when I called! We called the church pastor (a man) who was letting us use his building for tonight's message, and he also has been tolerating Jezebel...

Oh, wait, back up. I had a dream last night that there were around 200 people in the church where Kenny was preaching! This is powerful, because this little inner city church is blessed if there are maybe 30 people at a meeting. So, here is what we encountered:

1. This woman is living in funeral home
2. Found out tonight that in my past 7 years since I last saw her, she had a child through adultery with another preacher
3. she is beautiful and could be on a magazine cover

> Pro 9:18   But he does not know that the dead are there, that her guests are in the depths of hell.

כִּי־חַסְדְּךָ גָּדוֹל עָלָי וְהִצַּלְתָּ נַפְשִׁי מִשְּׁאוֹל תַּחְתִּיָּה For GREAT is Your mercy toward me - for You have delivered my soul from the depths of Sheol...Psalm 86

Her mask came off tonight. When I was enamored by lady prophetesses for a season, when I saw some of them actually submitted to their husbands and prophesying in their Biblical places of influence (like in their homes), I was drawn to this woman. She would hold meetings at a public schoolhouse, so I thought it was OK to join in, because it was not a church.

Well, tonight, Abba sent us Dave, a brother who ministers to street addicts and harlots, so he probably has better discernment than me. Kenny began his message on time (we knew we had to keep a step ahead of Jezebel - she did not outrun us tonight - remember Elijah how he had to outrun??) and about 15 minutes in, she waltzed in, dressed in black, drawing attention to herself and interrupting his message! "WHAT ARE you doing KENNY??!!"

Quite embarrassing...how would you feel if, when a preacher was giving the word, a woman walked in and treated him like a little disobedient child and scolded him? How does this look to newborn baby believers like the one that was with us tonight? Paul would have probably been VERY angry, like at the church in Corinth -

$\frac{1Cr}{3:3}$ ...for you are still carnal. For where there are envy, strife, and divisions among you, are you not carnal and behaving like mere men?

We tried to suffer long, but we had reached our limit! This previously grey area became VERY CLEARLY BLACK AND WHITE tonight - NO MORE!!! We left to go to McDonald's to have church there so Kenny could finish his message that was so rudely interrupted! And WOULD YOU BELIEVE THAT ONLY 1 PERSON STAYED WITH HER??? Hilarious - our stand for righteousness was backed by the congregation!

WHEW! And we even had permission to play guitar at the McDonald's and people were gladly receiving tracts and ministry and prayer! So our congregation GREW at the McDonald's!

We had to repent for letting ourselves be put under her spell - and wow was it a powerful one! Kenny himself admitted that he had been deceived - and that is what the WORD says - GREAT DECEPTION in the last days (1

Timothy 4). She was even promising to ordain Kenny - using the authority of the state - very similar to the woman who rides the beast in the book of revelation -

	So he carried me away in the Spirit into the
Rev	wilderness. And I saw a woman sitting on a scarlet
17:3	beast that was full of names of blasphemy, having
	seven heads and ten horns.

Some view this as the compromising churches in the last days "fornicating" with the godless civil governments of this world and accepting their authority over the authority of the WORD...like people who say they are ordained and can do marriages because of the STATE. What is your interpretation of this Scripture?

Kenny resisted this temptation and does not even WANT this ordination license if it means having to be under Jezebel! **Pray for Kenny and all of us OK?** I have to say I saw a real teaching gift in him, and our stand against the spiritual hosts of wickedness really causes the FIRE of Eloheem to fall! And NO I DO NOT HATE WOMEN...I love them (I am married to one.) But we as a ministry have ceased to TOLERATE JEZEBEL and her OPERATIONS OF DARKNESS.

How to destroy Jezebel spirit.

In the eleventh year of Joram the son of Ahab, Ahaziah had become king over Judah.

| **2Ki 9:30** | Now when Jehu had come to Jezreel, Jezebel heard [of it]; and she put paint on her eyes and adorned her head, and looked through a window. |

2Ki 9:31   Then, as Jehu entered at the gate, she said, "[Is it] peace, Zimri, murderer of your master?"

2Ki 9:32   And he looked up at the window, and said, "Who [is] on my side? Who?" So two [or] three eunuchs looked out at him.

2Ki 9:33   Then he said, "Throw her down." So they threw her down, and [some] of her blood spattered on the wall and on the horses; and he trampled her underfoot.

2Ki 9:34   And when he had gone in, he ate and drank. Then he said, "Go now, see to this accursed [woman], and bury her, for she was a king's daughter."

Notice that Jehu did not TALK TO THE DEMONS. I have notice in my head-on encounters with Jezebel that she feeds on attention. Have you ever made eye contact with a person, and just doing so DRAINED YOU of your spiritual vitality? I HAVE! In fact, I have warned my wife and other women when we have walked through strongholds of Islam to not look those murderous devils in the eyes. Spirits can transfer through the eye gates, and many of them feed on FEAR. If you show fear, you can be devoured very easily. Jezebel is now a DEMON spirit that we need to overcome. But TALKING TO HER can actually cause problems. DO NOT LET DEMONS EVEN SPEAK! This can just cause you all kinds of problems that you do not need. Learn to

1. BIND the spirits that are operating in people before you even enter their homes or churches
2. When a person manifests a demon, LOOSE the armor of light to help you and your deliverance team cast out the spirit from the person – if and only if they are ready to repent.

I was working with some of the homeless people in southern CA, and was once chosen by them to cast demons out of a street prostitute. They (homeless) were sleeping under a church awning with pastor's permission and this woman would come in the middle of the night and TORMENT the sleepers. We took a group to deal with this woman – though we quickly realized it was not her, but DEMONS operating in her. Who knows how many times SHE had been beaten and raped? Amazingly enough, it was not much of a battle…how? THE BLOOD OF THE LAMB. As the Sabbath began, and we were breaking bread and fellowshipping, and she came to our small group outside at the Orange Circle…the air was tense, because people knew I was there to cast out her demons. My friend actually said to her, 'Do you know about the blood of Yahshua יֵשׁוּעַ ?" and just the very mention of the blood COMPLETELY SUBDUED HER DEMONS! What a joy to see street prostitutes delivered and set free by the blood of Christ! Seeing them have their garments WASHED in the BLOOD / and they became WHITE as snow!

Receiving the TRUE prophetic gift could cut your missionary funding. I actually have a TRUE testimony of a pastor who worked with the church in Russia. I was young and ON FIRE when I received יְהֹוָה אֱלֹהִים and the baptism of the Spirit came later, and with me I began to speak in tongues. It even happened when I was sleeping ... I woke up to the sound of myself speaking in tongues! It kind of scared me because I was not used to something that powerful. I knew it was going to be a problem because I was raised in churches that teach that tongues is fleshly at best and demonic at worst. They say it does not operate any longer in the church. This is a false teaching that many MAJOR Bible scholars hold to! (This can happen when your Christianity is all up in your head.) At any rate, we went to Russia (my youth group) that summer after I was born again (2000). How exciting! We were hungry for the miraculous, and we experienced it! But, this was not too well received by the elders back home in the USA! Of course they wanted to hear about people being saved (born again), and I admit that that is the greatest miracle - a life transformed from darkness into light! HALLELUYAH! But when I later found out that the fire of the Holy Spirit caused this pastor's wife to receive the gift of tongues, our wealthy church FIRED them as supported missionaries! Suddenly, they dropped off of our missionary prayer lists and it was like HUSH HUSH when they were brought up! HOW AWFUL! It's enough that they are poor and our rich church in America was able to relieve some of that affliction by sending regular support, but to remove that blessing BECAUSE THEY RECEIVED A GIFT

FROM THE HOLY SPIRIT WAS LIKE ADDING
INSULT TO INJURY!!! Paul wrote, '

> 1Cr
> 14:5
>
> I wish you all spoke with tongues, but even more
> that you prophesied; for he who prophesies [is]
> greater than he who speaks with tongues, unless
> indeed he interprets, that the church may receive
> edification.

So, I guess what I am trying to say, is to count the cost
even of RECEIVING gifts from the Holy Spirit. I
remember coming home to the USA with that youth
group, and we were ABLAZE with testimonies - how our
pastor rebuked the psychic at the Russian national circus
and the forces of light came against the ones of darkness
and WON, how souls were saved through our dramatic
reenactment of the crucifixion, and so on. How
discouraging when the sleepy American church and some
of my believing family members received our report with
little interest.

Many of the spiritual gifts work together. Many times
you cannot experience these powerful manifestations of
the Holy Spirit until you put yourself into a vulnerable
position where יְהֹוָה אֱלֹהִים has to deliver you. As Heidi
Baker once said, 'If יְהֹוָה אֱלֹהִים does not show up, we are
DEAD.' Hungry for more international experiences, but
also to experience more of this mysterious 3rd person of
the FATHER - SON - HOLY SPIRIT of who יְהֹוָה
אֱלֹהִים is, I began raising support for my next mission trip
- Africa! (By the way, that Hebrew word for 'God'

includes all 3 - יְהוָה אֱלֹהִים) This time, since I was in training to become a physician, I found an OB/GYN who took teams of pre-medical students to the Central African Republic to deliver babies. So, this ministry was more focused in HEALING, another one of the Holy Spirit manifestations! I was excited, other than the fact that this mission board was ALSO not open to the Holy Spirit doing miracles and giving people the ability to prophesy and speak in tongues. BUT as Micah the prophet wrote, 'Is the Spirit of יְהוָה אֱלֹהִים restricted?' (Micah 2) We found ourselves on Nanga rock, and there were a bunch of young African children around us. So beautiful! Our Father is so creative in how He designed the DNA of each tribe, tongue and nation! Would you believe, as we went to love on these children, we were swarmed by African killer bees? These are some of the most aggressive bees - they land STINGER first! So, we were running and trying to escape. I was stung on the chin and it felt like I got punched in the face! The worst part about it, was my friend Matthew was stung about 17 times - AND HE WAS ALLERGIC TO BEESTINGS! This very easily could have killed him. We began to fervently pray. I fell to my knees, asking יְהוָה אֱלֹהִים for mercy. The physician leading the trip seemed to not know what to do. As we prayed more and more, the swelling went down, and he was healed! 'Physician, heal yourself,' like they told Yahshua יֵשׁוּעַ in the Bible! HA! But Yahshua יֵשׁוּעַ DID heal him! And what is even more amazing, is that we saw this was a spiritual attack! We went back to

75

the village where Nanga rock was, and climbed back up to find those children. A pastor who spoke their tribal dialect just happened to be walking by, and he translated our message, and 17 children received CHRIST! Truly a healing miracle from the Holy Spirit paved the way for the salvation of souls!

There are 9 manifestations of the Holy Spirit listed in 1 Corinthians 12, 'But the manifestation of the Spirit is given to each one for the profit of all:

1Cr 12:8	for to one is given the word of wisdom through the Spirit, to another the word of knowledge through the same Spirit,
1Cr 12:9	to another faith by the same Spirit, to another gifts of healings by the same Spirit,
1Cr 12:10	to another the working of miracles, to another prophecy, to another discerning of spirits, to another [different] kinds of tongues, to another the interpretation of tongues.'

I have seen them be stirred up and operating in a powerful way. For example, a word of knowledge that someone has a problem with their heart could lead to prayer for that individual, thus releasing healing anointing from the Holy Spirit. Or, a miracle could happen after someone prophesies that someone is going to raise from the dead. That is the beauty of the gifts - like intricately woven fabric on a beautiful dress, they are all weaved together and work strongest together. That is another reason why Paul says, 'Do not grieve the Holy Spirit, by whom you were sealed for the day of redemption.'

Anni – Jerusalem wedding 2010

What if you give a prophetic word, and you are persecuted!?

Expect it! Delight in it! Rejoice when it happens! It means you are on the narrow road that leads to life! In Jerusalem, we stepped on some toes of elders, but we had to prophetically oppose what they were doing, because they were letting unbelieving rabbis speak, and were more impressed by TITLE and EDUCATION than the work of the Holy Spirit who pours through ordinary street people and fishermen. So, to protect the innocent impressionable sheep (like the Americans) we took over! I gave a prophetic word during worship and did not ask for permission from the elders. I just know what His word says -

Let two or three prophets speak, and let the others judge.

1Cr 14:30

But if [anything] is revealed to another who sits by, let the first keep silent.

1Cr 14:31

For you can all prophesy one by one, that all may learn and all may be encouraged.

I felt His anointing on the WORD - the worship was RICH, and this act of boldness (I am boasting in Him) seemed to bring the Presence of the Father in a powerful way, but I was later told NOT TO COME BACK! So - just because people get angry at you and throw you out, DOESN'T MEAN you falsely prophesied! You probably did exactly what Abba wanted - many prophets have to confront behaviors that send churches into spiritual death - doing radical and dramatic things to WAKE PEOPLE UP!   How many times was Yahshua יֵשׁוּעַ almost run off of a cliff? Or Jeremiah thrown into prison for speaking truth? I know a man who went into the church of an abortion doctor, sat down, and when communion was passed to him, he said, "This is not that blood of Yahshua יֵשׁוּעַ , this is the blood of the unborn children whose slaughter you approve of by letting THAT MAN come to you church!" He ended up getting arrested...but HEY - we need to obey יְהֹוָה צְבָא ֹות rather than MAN.

Prophecy and politics.

This is an area that I personally am seeking to grow in. I saw a vision of a bear coming out of the water when I went to a men's retreat years ago to Montana. I was amazed to then read about this in the Bible! Daniel spoke, saying, "I saw in my vision by night, and behold, the four winds of heaven were stirring up the Great Sea.

Dan "And four great beasts came up from the sea, each
7:3 different from the other.

Dan "The first [was] like a lion, and had eagle's wings. I
7:4 watched till its wings were plucked off; and it was lifted up from the earth and made to stand on two feet like a man, and a man's heart was given to it.

Dan "And suddenly another beast, a second, like a bear. It
7:5 was raised up on one side, and [had] three ribs in its mouth between its teeth. And they said thus to it: 'Arise, devour much flesh!'

Some people told me that the bear is Russia but I received other confirming dreams that proved to me that it is also California. (Many of them and Americans are RAVENOUS meat eaters.) When you see that Abba speaks through prophets BEFORE Christ and then often speaks the same message AFTER Christ (read Revelation), you see that prophecy and political forces are clearly things that believers need to devote their attention to.

I also received a vision of a fishhook one year on an airplane as I was flying to Israel. This hook was pulling a burning map of Israel off of a page of paper FROM THE EAST and on the hook was an evangelist I know who is trapped in Israel. He slid down it and knocked the edge of the hook and fell onto Jerusalem.

Fascinating! I then learned about the threats of Iran and other Islamic nations to 'wipe Israel off of the map.' Also, the city of Jerusalem, though referred to as a harlot in the prophecy of Ezekiel, is referred to as a 'burdensome stone' by the prophet Zechariah. And it shall happen in that day that I will make Jerusalem a very heavy stone for all peoples; all who would heave it away will surely be cut in pieces, though all nations of the earth are gathered against it.

> Zec "In that day," says יְהוָה, "I will strike every horse with
> 12:4 confusion, and its rider with madness; I will open My eyes on the house of Judah, and will strike every horse of the peoples with blindness.

When Yahshua יֵשׁוּעַ warned His nation, what did He say? "Therefore I say to you, the kingdom of God will be taken from you and given to a nation bearing the fruits of it."

> Mat "And whoever falls on this stone will be broken;
> 21:44 but on whomever it falls, it will grind him to powder."

While for a season Abba removed His protection from Israel and allowed them to be plundered and crushed down, Jerusalem will again emerge in the last days as a city of truth, where righteousness dwells. The demonic agenda of Islam to mock the Creator will be EASILY destroyed when the Savior returns with the clouds to split the Mt. of Olives in two! They sealed the Eastern Gate (the very one prophesied that Yahshua יֵשׁוּעַ will return THROUGH) with a graveyard of DEAD MUSLIMS and with STONES so that people cannot physically walk through! Yuck!

Also an earthquake is prophesied to divide the city of Jerusalem into thirds, in Revelation. Then [those] from the peoples, tribes, tongues, and nations will see their dead bodies three-and-a-half days, and not allow their dead bodies to be put into graves.

Rev 11:10   And those who dwell on the earth will rejoice over them, make merry, and send gifts to one another, because these two prophets tormented those who dwell on the earth.

Rev 11:11   Now after the three-and-a-half days the breath of life from God entered them, and they stood on their feet, and great fear fell on those who saw them.

Rev 11:12   And they heard a loud voice from heaven saying to them, "Come up here." And they ascended to heaven in a cloud, and their enemies saw them.

Rev 11:13   In the same hour there was a great earthquake, and a tenth of the city fell. In the earthquake seven thousand people were killed, and the rest were afraid and gave glory to אֱלֹהֵי הַשָּׁמַיִם .

This is an earthquake in response to the murder of the two prophets who will prophesy clothed in sackcloth in Israel for 3.5 years. Father answers when His prophets get hurt! And He kills people in His anger....

How about Revelation 16 - Then the seventh angel poured out his bowl into the air, and a loud voice came out of the temple of heaven, from the throne, saying, "It is done!"

Rev   And there were noises and thunderings and lightnings; and there was a great earthquake, such a

<u>16:18</u>   mighty and great earthquake as had not occurred
since men were on the earth.

<u>Rev</u>   Now the great city was divided into three parts, and
<u>16:19</u>   the cities of the nations fell. And great Babylon was
remembered before אֶל־הַיְם, to give her the cup of the
wine of the fierceness of His wrath.

I have heard major preachers say before large audiences that
Jerusalem is the 'eternal undivided capital of Israel.' In light of this
prophecy, I do not agree!

But to get back to prophecy and politics, I have to confess my own
failures! I have TRIED based on prophetic dreams to try and get
candidates into office who I knew were born again without
succeeding. I worked with others, prayed and fasted and it did not
happen! Some would say that demonic authorities HAVE to get into
these high ranking political positions because prophecy has to be
fulfilled in Revelation involving the antichrist, beast and false
prophet, but I have heard others say that we need end times Daniels,
Josephs and Esthers to rise up! WHAT IS THE TRUTH???

I have noticed, however, that women tend to have a false optimism
that often manifests as FALSE PROPHECY in this arena. In fact, in
my zeal upon return to USA to get Obama out of office, I
misinterpreted a Scripture and ran with it to a large email
audience! This also happened when a politician misquoted the
prophet Isaiah after 9/11 - "The bricks have fallen down, But
we will rebuild with hewn stones; The sycamores are cut
down, But we will replace [them] with cedars." Isaiah 9:10.
This man failed to read the verse before..."All the people will
know--Ephraim and the inhabitant of Samaria--Who say in
pride and arrogance of heart" v. 9! The rebuilding he was
referring to was a move motivated by pride and rebellion

against the Creator, much like the tower of Babel! (Read <u>The Harbinger</u> by Jonathan Cahn for more information about this.) But he spoke about it as though it was a heroic move that Abba had blessed! I guess we will see what happens.

I guess my conclusion is this - IF YAHSHUA יֵשׁוּעַ TAUGHT US TO PRAY THAT HIS KINGDOM COME AND HIS WILL BE DONE ON EARTH AS IT IS IN HEAVEN, WHY ARE WE NOT TAKING THE KINGDOM BY FORCE when it comes to politics, and really ALL FIELDS for that matter?

Prophecy takes TIME. We are to JUDGE prophecy (1 Corinthians 14), but Yahshua יֵשׁוּעַ warned us also. He said that we reap what we sow and also to be merciful as your heavenly Father is merciful. Those of us who are quick to judge often reap of that same kind of behavior from others in the body of Christ. I have made this mistake a number of times. I came down very hard on someone who gave word that may not have contained full truth, only to find out that they were right.

The example that comes to mind is when a lady with the gift of prophecy told me that demons were telling me to fast. I was initially offended and thought, 'Demons do not tell people to fast!' Sure enough, her message to me rang true when I was overseas and learned about anorexia. This is a demonic spirit (1 Timothy 4). In our swiftness to judge someone else's prophetic dream, sometimes we need to slow down and wait. Jeremiah was accused of being a false prophet because he said that the captivity in Babylon would be LONG (70 years). Daniel's prophetic words were spoken thousands of years before they came to pass!

My experience in the realm of politics and prophecy is that Abba will reveal His will, by prophetic dreams or other ways.

The prophets are to then sound the alarm, and if the people do not choose Abba's will, the prophetic people are free from bloodguilt. Their hands are free from blood. If you are a prophetic person, you have done your job, and many times, until you have done it, you will feel like a woman in travail!

This is also true of abortion. If you KNOW someone is threatening to murder their child, you are the one Abba has chosen to counsel this friend out of a bad decision. Do it! Do you care more about what your friend thinks about you, or what Abba thinks about you? When I have seen one person stand up for what is right, and risk social rejection, I have been SO BLESSED by that one! That one I really respected more than the people who always GO WITH THE FLOW, socially.

This recent election (2012), I was comforted by a number of Scriptures. I felt helpless because I did not know what to do or how to help, so many times I just knelt down and prayed, tears streaming down my face. AMERICA HAS BEEN WEIGHED IN THE SCALES AND FOUND WANTING. My wife and I stood outside of a political rally and gave out fliers revealing what Abba showed me by prophetic dream. Another woman was VERY strong on convincing people to pass pro-life legislation. We felt like Paul when he visited Macedonia

2Cr 7:5   For indeed, when we came to Macedonia, our bodies had no rest, but we were troubled on every side. Outside [were] conflicts, inside [were] fears.

But, through the Scripture, I was comforted. Even our Father cries like a woman sometimes when we make bad decisions!!!

Isa   "I have held My peace a long time, I have been still and

85

<u>42:14</u> restrained Myself. [Now] I will cry like
a woman in labor, I will pant and gasp at once.

IF THERE ARE SO MANY CHRISTIANS IN AMERICA, WHY
ARE SO MANY OF THEM SEEMINGLY NOT CHOOSING
RIGHTEOUSNESS, PEACE AND JOY IN THE HOLY SPIRIT??
With death it seems they are in agreement, and PROUD OF IT!! The
prophet Isaiah hit the nail on the head

> Because you have said, "We have made a
> covenant with death, And with Sheol we are in
>
> Isa agreement. When the overflowing scourge passes
> 28:15 through, It will not come to us, For we have made lies
> our refuge, And under falsehood we have hidden
> ourselves."

> Your covenant with death will be annulled, And your
> Isa agreement with Sheol will not stand; When the
> 28:18 overflowing scourge passes through, Then you will be
> trampled down by it.

Way to go America! 2012! I also opened to this in Acts:

Now Herod had been very angry with the people of Tyre and
Sidon; but they came to him with one accord, and having made
Blastus the king's personal aide their friend, they asked for
peace, because their country was supplied with food by the
king's [country].

<u>Act</u>   So on a set day Herod, arrayed in royal

12:21	apparel, sat on his throne and gave an oration to them.
Act 12:22	And the people kept shouting, "The voice of a god and not of a man!"
Act 12:23	Then immediately an angel of the אֲדֹנָי יְהוִה struck him, because he did not give glory to יְהוִה אֲדֹנָי . And he was eaten by worms and died.
Act 12:24	But the word of יְהוִה אֲדֹנָי grew and multiplied.

It was as though the Holy Spirit was saying to me, between my sobs, 'I have the power to kill and the power to heal. I am SO MUCH GREATER than the political systems of the USA.'

I also received a WORD about the Republican party - "Surely, when the wall has fallen, will it not be said to you, 'Where [is] the mortar that you plastered [it] with?'

Eze 13:13	Therefore thus says יְהוִה אֲדֹנָי : "I will cause a stormy wind to break forth in My fury; and there shall be a flooding rain in My anger, and great hailstones in fury to consume [it].

I mean, would Abba REALLY want a cult member (Mormon) as the head of our nation?

Prophecy and marriage. I have heard a number of people who say not to prophesy marriages. Having recently been ordained and having done a wedding, I know that marriage is not a very black and white area. Let's look at the instruction the prophet Hosea received from יְהוָה - Therefore I will uncover your skirts over your face, that your shame may appear.

Jer   I have seen your adulteries And your [lustful]
13:27   neighings, The lewdness of your harlotry, Your
        abominations on the hills in the fields. Woe to you, O
        Jerusalem! Will you still not be made clean?"

Jerusalem had reached an all-time low. The city that Zechariah prophesied would be a 'city of truth' in the last days in whom righteousness dwells, had been acting like a harlot. Abba was SO heartbroken that His bride had forsaken His law, and covenant, that He needed a prophet who He could pour out His soul to. He chose Hosea!

Hsa 1:2   When יְהֹוָה began to speak by Hosea, יְהֹוָה said to
          Hosea: "Go, take yourself a wife of harlotry And
          children of harlotry, For the land has committed
          great harlotry [By departing] from יְהֹוָה."

Many times prophecy is given as a general instruction, and Abba entrusts to us the specifics of it. This is probably because He is our Father and He likes to give us freedom to choose. What did Hosea do?

Hsa 1:3   So he went and took Gomer the daughter of
          Diblaim, and she conceived and bore him a son.

He was given the OPTION! Here is where a number of believers misunderstand FREEDOM in Christ. When Abba speaks to His children, and He is giving a command, He then the details up to us. We are not robots. (The occult turns you into a robot.) Yahshua יֵשׁוּעַ said, 'You are My friends if you keep My commands' (

<u>John 15:10</u> "If you keep My commandments, you will abide in
My love, just as I have kept My Father's
commandments and abide in His love.)

This recently happened to us, and we are also in the middle of a
prophetic instruction. Abba said He wants 100 homes dedicated and
consecrated with mezuzahs on the doorposts and on the gates - we
are sounding the alarm. Our testimony is that when we took ours
down in our prayer room - apartment in Finland, DEMONS
SOMEHOW GAINED ACCESS TO OUR DWELLING PLACE .
The persecution in America is going to increase as the love of many
waxes cold. If we desire the gift of prophecy, we need to be careful
not to reject Abba's discipline in our lives. We also need to NOT BE
ASHAMED OF THE HOLY SPIRIT, the gospel or the utterance of
the Spirit.

This leads me to the next area - we were led by a prophetic vision to
a shopping mall - I saw 2 women - one was swinging her head
looking to the other one. I knew we were to go and share the gospel
at the mall. I told Anni exactly what we were looking for - I saw a
headband on one of them - and would you believe, as we made
diligent search, WE FOUND THEM! One had an eating disorder
(our ministry anointing and calling - Naphtali Services
www.wrestlewithyah.webs.com) and was not born again. What
resulted from our obedience was one of the most powerful blessings
of the Spirit in my own personal prayer times and my wife and I
being directed supernaturally in our prophetic calling that many
people misunderstand.

<u>John 15:10</u> "If you keep My commandments, you will abide in
My love, just as I have kept My Father's
commandments and abide in His love.

As you deepen in your intimacy with the Bridegroom, Yahshua יֵשׁוּעַ (Jesus Christ of Nazareth), He will begin to direct you supernaturally and help you to 'abide in His love.'

But, back to the prophet Hosea, and marriage. The counsel we have received from the Holy Spirit for the generation of sodomites that we live among, is that Abba is calling people who have been involved in homosexual behaviors, after they are born again, to get married in a heterosexual union. He is using such people as a prophetic witness AGAINST these devils and their doctrines (1 Timothy 4). Is Abba calling you to marriage? If you have a past involvement in homosexuality, really fast and pray for His perfect will. You do not want to end up in deeper bondage, and you need to live in a nurturing community that will help you work through many of the psychological struggles that often manifest in people with such pasts.

Also, find a good pastor who is merciful as our Father in heaven is! So, with prophecy and marriage, BE VERY CAREFUL. I know of a number of people who have falsely prophesied, in the area. Let me give you some horror stories (they are true):

1. A woman who was born again whose mother was a prostitute and was really catching the fire of the Spirit did not fully understand the self-control aspect of the Spirit and had sex with someone after she was publicly baptized in a revival.
2. An ex-drag queen who published a DVD with his testimony kept falling back into sexual sin with other men (said he was born again)
3. I know of a man in Christ who decided to inform a woman that the Holy Spirit said they were to get married.-- this scared her, and she ended up marrying an African and leaving this man hanging and in confusion because he was SO SURE the Holy Spirit told him...

These are just 3 that come to mind, and I am SURE there are hundreds or thousands more. The key to prophecy and marriage I think is found in Hosea. Abba instructs and then gives us freewill to choose (though not always - think of how Abraham sent a servant to find a wife for Isaac - Isaac had NO SAY in the matter - I also knew a Russian pastor whose marriage was arranged and it ended up being a BLESSING for him - technically it IS somewhat biblical to have NO SAY and there are other cases -

If a man entices a virgin who is not betrothed, and lies with her, he shall surely pay the bride-price for her [to be] his wife.

Exd 22:17

"If her father utterly refuses to give her to him, he shall pay money according to the bride-price of virgins.

) To be honest, I have only been married 2 years and am far from being the expert! My personal testimony is that I was commanded by Eloheem אֱלֹהִים to marry it was black and white and my life was not promised if I did not obey and when I found a lovely Finnish woman in Jerusalem at the Feast of Tabernacles and took this great step of faith, Abba then on the other side of my obedience EXTENDED my life by prophetic word. AND said, '

Psa 118:23 This was the LORD's doing; It [is] marvelous in our eyes.

Lexicon / Concordance for Psalms 118:23

91

118:23

מֵאֵת יְהוָה הָיְתָה זֹּאת הִיא נִפְלָאת בְּעֵינֵ ֫ינוּ׃

There is more to be honest regarding financial blessing on the other side of this commitment and obedience, but THAT IS NONE OF YOUR BUSINESS!

So, in conclusion, when it comes to prophecy and marriage, work out your own salvation with fear and trembling...do not be so prophetic that you miss practical wisdom that comes from family, and from elders and people who have by the experience of marriage - WISDOM.

Prophets are often called to do strange things...Moses married a foreign woman! Then Miriam and Aaron spoke against Moses because of the Ethiopian woman whom he had married; for he had married an Ethiopian woman.

Num
12:2
So they said, "Has יְהוָה indeed spoken only through Moses? Has He not spoken through us also?" And יְהוָה heard [it].

Num
12:3
(Now the man Moses [was] very humble, more than all men who [were] on the face of the earth.)

Num
12:4
Suddenly יְהוָה said to Moses, Aaron, and Miriam, "Come out, you three, to the tabernacle of meeting!" So the three came out.

Num
12:5
Then יְהוָה came down in the pillar of cloud and stood [in] the door of the tabernacle, and called Aaron and Miriam. And they both went forward.

Num 12:6	Then He said, "Hear now My words: If there is a prophet among you, [I], יְהוָה, make Myself known to him in a vision; I speak to him in a dream.
Num 12:7	Not so with My servant Moses; He [is] faithful in all My house.
Num 12:8	I speak with him face to face, Even plainly, and not in dark sayings; And he sees the form of יְהוָה. Why then were you not afraid To speak against My servant Moses?"
Num 12:9	So the anger of יְהוָה was aroused against them, and He departed.

Here we see a warning to people of faith. If Abba calls one of your family members to marry someone from a different nation, do not complain. You could be smitten with leprosy! Abba does not have the same agenda that we do. One of the dangers of living in your own little bubble where you only accept white people, or people with dark skin, or Jewish people, is that you miss the bigger picture of what Abba is trying to do. He is in the business of redeeming men from every tribe, tongue and nation unto Himself by the blood of His Son! This is why Yahshua יֵשׁוּעַ was such an affront to His own, who did not receive Him. He was preparing His 12 apostles to go to all nations with His gospel.

Moses, who enjoyed such intimate friendship with יְהוָה as most prophets do, was prophesying by his marriage to a foreigner our Father's heart! But Miryam and Aharon seemed to give in to the 'Jewish pride' that still operates among Jews today (especially the unbelievers). In fact, my wife and I were walking along the beach in Tel Aviv at the close of a Sabbath, and I actually overheard a Jewish woman say, 'When my daughter was seeing a Gentile, I would not even let him in the house.'

The tone she said it in made me want to vomit! יְהֹוָה hates pride! Interestingly enough, Paul the Jewish apostle, turned the statement around on his own people who were stubbornly refusing the truth of the gospel and still preaching circumcision.

Phl	Beware of dogs, beware of evil workers, beware of the
3:2	mutilation!

But, we need to understand more this account in Numbers, about Moses and his sister and brother. I have often tried to tell MY sister and brother that I want us to be like that - a prophetic 3-fold chord. I even went to the wilderness like Moses to fast and pray...My desire to be prophetic was so strong that Abba was bound by His Word to bless me! In the wilderness, I had a vision of a woman who became a spiritual mother to me in the prophetic and in the discerning of spirits gift that she operates in. I was very intent on receiving His instruction, and though I did not return with stone tablets engraved by Father's finger, I was still very blessed by this commitment to fast and pray.

I have also seen powerful repentance by a wilderness fasting experience on Oahu. I made a vow to fast in the wilderness and Abba brought me there - on the mountain, though weary, and being attacked by demons (it happened to Yahshua יֵשׁוּעַ), I completed my vow...Abba brought to me a prophet and his wife (very older man) who had a vision of Gabriel. Gabriel, the angel who announced the birth of Messiah Yahshua יֵשׁוּעַ through the virgin Mary, also appeared to this prophet. Being elders, they were concerned about me, only around 26 at the time. Why was this young man in the wilderness fasting so much, and where was his family?

They tried to get me to come down - but I had made a fasting vow and was intent on finishing what I started! I have learned about wisdom with true fasting (Isaiah 58 - the heart of true missions) since the experience, but out of it came fruit that to this day remains. In fact, my friend Ken, also an elder, ended up moving to Israel and doing some powerful ministry and prophetic works with his wife in Israel and Jordan. Abba has this way of connecting us in Jerusalem at times that we need to see each other - very powerful!

And speaking of Jerusalem and marriage - that is where my foreign wife and I were married years later! So, WHO you marry can actually be a prophetic word - I found it interesting that my wife, having suffered a famine in her nation (Finland) was brought to America, a nation where people are overfed (one of the sins of Sodom). It seems Abba was trying to show mercy on BOTH SIDES - getting MY nation to eat less and HERS to eat more. (The reason they had famine was revealed to us by 2 prophetic visions - the first was a vision of a scorpion that had decapitated my wife with its tail - I knew there was a spirit of death trying to destroy my wife. (Don't worry – she is currently with my family AWAY from Finland.) Later, I saw a vision of a cornucopia like what you see at Thanksgiving only the cornucopia was like a shofar. I put the pieces of the puzzle together and realized how much Finnish people complain instead of giving thanks - OUR NATION HAS BEEN BLESSED WITH FOOD BECAUSE WE ARE SO THANKFUL!)

And now speaking again of Jerusalem - please read this written by my friend who is in Jerusalem and is seeing firsthand the war that is surrounding that city:

'The sirens just went off again in Jerusalem less than an hour ago (at 2:08 PM). Immediately following that the Muslims started their recorded chantings from the minarets. (From my view atop Mt. Scopus I can hear and see what is happening in the city below me.) Now we know for sure that there is war in their hearts. David said; "I

am for peace; but when I speak, they are for war." Ps. 120:7
Remember, George and Whitney, when those taxi drivers said "we
want work" but I heard "we want war" and I asked them about that -
by saying to them; *you want war*?
This latest event is confirmation of what is in the hearts of so many
Muslims in Jerusalem - or this would not have happened.
When the sirens go off, I don't go to the bomb shelter - rather I open
my window and look out over the city and pray for it.'
Obadiah 1:12

Oba 1:12 "But you should not have gazed on the day of your
brother In the day of his captivity; Nor should you have
rejoiced over the children of Judah In the day of their
destruction; Nor should you have spoken proudly In the
day of distress.

Isa 3:11 Woe to the wicked! [It shall be] ill [with him], For the
reward of his hands shall be given him.

Psa 121:4 Behold, He who keeps Israel Shall neither slumber nor
sleep.

By the way, a simple test of a false prophet is DID THEY DIE IN
JERUSALEM? This quickly eliminates probably half of the
Americans who said they were prophets (Joseph Smith – founder of
the Mormon heresy, died in Missouri). Yahshua יֵשׁוּעַ said,

Luk 13:33 "Nevertheless I must journey today, tomorrow, and the
[day] following; for it cannot be that a prophet should perish outside
of Jerusalem.

Luk 21:20 "But when you see Jerusalem surrounded by armies, then
know that its desolation is near.

Symbols in dreams and visions and what they possibly mean.

<u>Hsa 12:10</u> I have also spoken by the prophets, And have multiplied visions; I have given **symbols** through the witness of the prophets."

There a number of symbols in dreams and visions to look for, as messages that Abba may be speaking to you. Here are a few:

Spiders – craftiness, can be witchcraft or fear but not always (I saw a vision of an angel with a spider (probably symbolic of a spirit of witchcraft) and the caregiver of the widow confessed that her granddaughter had been dappling in the occult. I told her to destroy the objects in her home that were occultic and lay hands on this young woman and tell Satan to leave!

<u>Pro 30:28</u> The **spider** skillfully grasps with its hands, And it is in kings' palaces.

Cats – I have had a number of dreams about cats and these have often come to pass in the natural. Strife, spirits of distraction. I have seen many times specifically how animals pull the saints out of deep prayer times. One dream that comes to mind was when a cat was outside and my mother was inside the house (in the dream). Something was attacking her and yet I somehow got pulled out of the house by a cat (distraction).

Cows – women who are living in careless ease (like rich American women) and who oppress the poor

<u>Amo 4:1</u>   Hear this word, you cows of Bashan, who [are] on the mountain of Samaria, Who oppress the poor, Who crush the needy, Who say to your husbands, "Bring [wine], let

us drink!"

Dogs – Jews who preach circumcision and the law as a means of righteousness before Eloheem

Fruit – judgment, harvest of souls

Thus יְהוִה אֲדֹנָי showed me: Behold, a basket of summer fruit.

Amo 8:2 And He said, "Amos, what do you see?" So I said, "A basket of summer fruit." Then יְהוִה אֲדֹנָי said to me: "The end has come upon My people Israel; I will not pass by them anymore.

Moldy bread – dead works, hoarding, stinginess, distrust

A dirty house – a person in need of deliverance A clean house – a person who has received deliverance and is now filled with the Holy Spirit

Trees – healing (leaves) and people who are firmly rooted and grounded in the WORD

Money – people who need to be taken out of sinful lives, souls of men

Scorpion – lesbian spirit, spirit of lust or perversion (I saw a vision of a woman in Jerusalem who turned into a scorpion) My wife recently discerned a spirit that became violent and abusive through touch. Some spirits (especially sexual) manifest through physical touch (be careful).

Snake – tribe of Dan, wise as a serpent, also a spirit of perversion

Frog – unclean spirits including false prophecy, homosexual spirit, spirits that talk too much, fear, greed, lying signs and a spirit of adultery

Fire – purification, the Holy Spirit baptism

Water – refreshing, and the Holy Spirit

John 7:37   On the last day, that great [day] of the feast, Yahshua יֵשׁוּעַ stood and cried out, saying, "If anyone thirsts, let him come to Me and drink.

Colors (I personally believe that colors can mean different things to different people and the Holy Spirit knows how to speak to each of us, but here are suggestions)

Blue (see Numbers 15),

Num 15:38   "Speak to the children of Israel: Tell them to make tassels on the corners of their garments throughout their generations, and to put a blue thread in the tassels of the corners.

Purple – royalty

Red – the blood of the Lamb, war

Pale green – the spirit of Islam, the spirit of false accusation (I once received a vision of a kitchen in an African American church in southern CA and a HUGE DEMONIC LOOKING PALE GREEN FINGER WAS pointing at me. I noticed that in wisdom as my mother said years ago I needed to stay OUT of that kitchen!)

Rev 6:8   So I looked, and behold, a pale horse. And the name of him who sat on it was Death, and Hades followed with him. And power was given to them over a fourth of the earth, to kill with sword, with hunger, with death, and by the beasts of the earth.

(the Greek word for 'pale' is χλωρός *chlōros* and that chemical turns your hair pale green. Is this a prophecy about chemical warfare in addition to the spirit of Islam?) I learned about this one by a revelation from the Holy Spirit. I saw a vision of a green glow stick in my mouth. To me personally it was a warning from the Holy Spirit that

Pro 18:21 Death and life [are] in the power of the tongue, **And** those who love it will eat its fruit.

My tongue was being used to speak death instead of life! We must be careful what we say…

Black – poverty, death

Something I learned in Kansas City is how to use symbols in visions or dreams in evangelism. They called it 'treasure hunting.' This is where you pray in the Spirit before going to share your faith and you ask for words of knowledge and symbols to lead you in the ministry you do.

100

Hsa 12:10   I have also spoken by the prophets, And have multiplied visions; I have given symbols through the witness of the prophets."

I have greatly enjoyed this – a friend of mine once by telephone told me that I would encounter a woman wearing a certain kind of scarf necklace whom I was to minister to. Another friend of mine (Ezekiel) once said I would find a woman wearing a green shirt who spoke Spanish with children. We went to Aldi's AND THERE WAS THE EXACT WOMAN! I was almost on the floor in awe of

יְהֹוָה So specific! But that is our Father. Truly all the good works in evangelism are prepared in advance! And you may

not believe this, but I also received a word that Abba יְהֹוָה was going to fill our gas tank with 10 dollars. As we were driving back and praying in the Spirit, I felt the still small voice of the Spirit tell me to pull into a gas station. THAT GAS TANK WAS PREPAY AND SOMEONE PUT EXACTLY $10 ON THE PUMP! It had to have been an angel? But I am telling you, if you do not use the gift of the Holy Spirit and His 9 manifestations in street evangelism, you are really missing out!

Prophetic assignments are not always easy. Case and point – Hosea had to marry a prostitute. Ezekiel was forced to lay on his side. '"For I have laid on you the years of their iniquity, according to the number of the days, three hundred and ninety days; so you shall bear the iniquity of the house of Israel.

| **Eze 4:6** | "And when you have completed them, lie again on your right side; then you shall bear the iniquity of the house of Judah forty days. I have laid on you a day for each year. |

I was once given an exhortation to sleep in a car of a friend of mine (to identify more with the homeless). Anni and I were exhorted to cut off our hair and burn some with fire (see Ezekiel 5). We often have seen the fruits of our obedience, but other times things remain a mystery. One thing I know having done kingdom work in persecuted places is that sometimes Abba wants to change the appearance of His prophets to protect them. I also see the importance of receiving hospitality if you are a travelling evangelist or prophet. Many people are needing you to stay with them! Just as much as you are needing them to help you weather the storms of life. Often if you are prophetic a dream will be released to you in a place that is a rhema word of correction or edification for that family. I once stayed with a friend from IHOP and Abba gave me a dream of him as a baby and he was surrounded by different kinds of grain. I submitted the dream for interpretation to elders, and what was revealed is that different kinds of grain in a dream are different nations. This man had a calling to the nations! Anni and I also once stayed with an elderly woman, and we both received spiritual communication, both given a dream that was one and the same (Eloheem does this with husbands and wives many times.) In HER dream, her family was fighting over an olive tree (symbolic of Israel – Romans 11) and the fight caused a shaking of 3 or 4 olives off of the tree. Have you read Isaiah 17? It shall be as when the harvester gathers the grain, And reaps the heads with his arm; It shall be as he who gathers heads of grain In the Valley of Rephaim.

102

Isa 17:6   Yet gleaning grapes will be left in it, Like the shaking of an olive tree, Two [or] three olives at the top of the uppermost bough, Four [or] five in

its most fruitful branches," Says יְהֹוָה

אֱלֹהֵי of Israel.

Wow! Almost the exact prophecy revealed to Isaiah! My dream carried almost the same theme and helped direct us – the same night…I think it is key when you are going to a place to help in the ministry of the gospel to have an open date book.

Psa 81:10

I [am] אֱלֹהֶיךָ יְהֹוָה, Who brought you out of the land of Egypt; Open your mouth wide, and I will fill it.

Abba may have a plan for you – to stay with a single mother or even a family who is very poor, but He may also send you to a farmer or a family that needs the blessing of a child and you can pray for the womb of the mother to open. Be open and go

places with joy and anticipation of what אֱלֹהֶיךָ יְהֹוָה will do for you and for those to whom He is sending you. Do not be high-minded. Paul wrote,

Rom 12:16   Be of the same mind toward one another. Do not set your mind on high things, but associate with the humble. Do not be wise in your own opinion.

Also, remember what the Savior said,

Mat 10:41 "He who receives a **prophet** in the name of
a **prophet** shall receive a **prophet's reward**. And he who receives a
righteous man in the name of a righteous man shall receive a
righteous man's **reward**.

You could actually deprive someone of a reward if you do not
visit them! I believe it can actually grieve the Spirit when we
are demanding of the best hotels and require too much
maintenance in gospel travels…Abba actually spoke to me
about this in a dream, when I was in Finland. I had been
warned about a TV preacher a number of times in dreams.
Small problem – Anni and I were travelling around with him
on his ministry staff! UH OH…But in this dream, we were in
probably the most fancy, expensive hotel in Finland. I was
looking out from over the balcony of the room to see a small
swimming pool. I was then luring children into water for
baptism. THIS DREAM CAME TO PASS, but we had to
work around the selfish leadership in order for these two
young Finnish children to be baptized…

While on the topic of WHERE you stay, here is a recent
Jerusalem testimony (2012). A friend of mine from PA and
my wife and I were seeking Abba on WHERE to stay. I went
in the morning to talk to Abba, and found all kinds of bread
(Israelis do not like wasting bread and leave it in bags around
the time of the feasts – probably keeping the law of Moses

Lev 19:9 'When you reap the harvest of your land, you shall not
wholly reap the corners of your field, nor shall you gather
the **gleanings** of your harvest.

At any rate, I saw a brother in Messiah, and he prayed and
quickly felt a leading from the Spirit that we needed to come to

his youth hostel in a different part of the city. We obeyed, and ended up being stuffed like sardines in a sardine can! 4 of us (2 married couples) stuffed into one room, and it REEKED of marijuana or some kind of smoked drug. They put my friend from PA on the roof! But, through it all, the anointing for evangelism fell. It was run by Muslims! Talk about scary! But, we began to share the word – I talked to a Jew, and then, a Korean youth, and she later was found talking to my wife. SHE WAS STARVING FOR THE BREAD OF LIFE. In her Jerusalem pilgrimage, she found the only Savior of the WORLD – Yahshua יֵשׁוּעַ ! She prayed to receive HIM! And after, when I went back to our room, a flood of peace filled my soul…we had been through all that difficulty because Abba is in the business of seeking and saving the lost.

So do not complain if you are wondering WHY you are in an unpleasant living situation. Think of people who are in prison cells for their faith in places like Bhutan, and India…who daily risk their lives to bring the BREAD OF LIFE to the spiritually starving peoples and tribes and tongues around them. Abba has you there for a reason…

Numbers and dreams – This is an area where false prophecy mixes in very easily. I have not arrived when it comes to this subject matter. The Jews are often quick to be superstitious about these kinds of things, and Christians can also fall prey to this (I have in the past.) Again, just like the colors, these are not all necessarily biblical, just what I have heard. Be careful too, because the Jews use a book of witchcraft called the Kabbalah that goes by numerology…

5 – the number of grace

7 – rest, completion

8 – new beginnings (Shimnei atzeret – the 8th day of the Feast of Tabernacles is when the Jews traditionally roll the torah scroll back to Genesis and the law of Moses also says 'And Moses commanded them, saying: "At the end of [every] seven years, at the appointed time in the year of release, at the Feast of Tabernacles,

Deu 31:11 "when all Israel comes to appear before יְהוָה

אֶל הֶיךָ in the place that He chooses, you shall read this law before all Israel in their hearing.'

This was also the day that Yahshua יְשׁוּעַ said 'If anyone thirsts, let him come to Me and drink' (John 7:37).

666 – the mark of the beast (in my early days in Christ, I would say that my 'lucky number' was 212. I was in a University class one day after my born again experience, and was randomly typing on my calculator. I typed in 666 / 212 and the answer is Pi - 3.1415... I was amazed, especially because Revelation says, '

Rev 13:18 Here is wisdom. Let him who has understanding **calculate** the number of the beast, for it is the number of a man: His number [is] 666.)

Did you know, 3:33 is God's phone number?

<u>Jer 33:3</u> 'Call to Me, and I will answer you, and show you great and mighty things, that you do not know.'

Remember the prophetic dream that Pharaoh received?

<u>Gen 41:3</u> Then behold, seven other **cows** came up after them out of the river, ugly and gaunt, and stood by the [other] **cows** on the bank of the river.

<u>Gen 41:4</u> And the ugly and gaunt **cows** ate up the seven fine looking and fat **cows**. So Pharaoh awoke.

Remember Joseph's interpretation?

<u>Gen 41:26</u> "The seven good **cows** [are] seven years

So the number of something is key in dream interpretation. Also, Daniel's prophecy about the weeks of years that was coincident with the arrival of the Messiah in Jerusalem! On a donkey! I remember entering into a time of fasting years ago, and Abba answered my prayer about the length of my days through a license plate! Then He confirmed it through a prophecy that a Finnish youth spoke on the Sabbath when my wife and I were ministering in Finland. He had spoken the same message in a peculiar way through 2 totally detached sources. He often will do that – to REALLY drive a point home. Notice that the dream that Pharaoh received was a message from יְהוָה צְבָא֫וֹת given to teach his nation to PREPARE. And I can see that we (saints living in America) are also needing to prepare for things that are coming. Persecution, famine and other afflictions that are common to other nations and that Americans have not really ever experienced in severe measure ARE ALL COMING as a result of continual grievance to the Holy Spirit and Abba's wrath ready to be revealed in the last day (see Romans 2 and Revelation). America's rebellion against His will in the election, in abortion and abominable gay marriage are just fuel for HIS judgment fires that have already begun to be poured out over FIRST the house of Eloheem. Our nation is in need of TRUE prophets now more than ever before and we are in need of EARS TO HEAR WHAT IS THE HOLY SPIRIT SAYING. As Ray Comfort wrote in all his wisdom, 'Praise

יְהֹוָה and pass the ammunition!'

Prophetic excess. True prophets are persecuted, and I would say even more so than other believers.

Hbr 11:37 They were stoned, they were sawn in two, were tempted, were slain with the sword. They wandered about in sheepskins and goatskins, being destitute, afflicted, tormented--

WOW! How would you feel about that happening to you? In America, this is almost unheard of (unless you count unborn children as prophets – murdered in the womb through abortion), but not so in other nations. Have you read, 'Tortured for Christ' by Richard Wurmbrand? Here is another Scripture:

Luk 11:49 "Therefore the wisdom of God also said, 'I will send them prophets and apostles, and [some] of them they will kill and persecute,'

Also, Babylon is said to be avenged by the Father because of the Jezebel spirit persecuting the apostles and prophets:

Rev 18:20   "Rejoice over her, O heaven, and [you] holy
                 apostles and prophets, for God has avenged you on her!"

So, when true prophets come, they have a message of comfort, edification and exhortation for the true sheep. One thing I have learned about true prophets is that they are often being hunted – perhaps by an anti-missionary organization such as Yad Lacheem in Israel, or perhaps by elders from the Mormon church that they are exposing or by an abortion clinic they have been preaching against. Remember Corrie ten Boom, who protected Jews during the Holocaust? Or how about Obadiah who hid the prophets of Yah in a cave feeding them with bread and water during the persecutions of Jezebel? Keeping prophets in one place for too long is not good! For EITHER party. Prophecy, and speaking in tongues, brings edification. It builds you up. BUT TOO MUCH OF A GOOD THING IS NOT GOOD!

Pro 25:16   Have you found honey? Eat only as much as you need,
                 Lest you be filled with it and vomit.

Prophecy is like honey. Paul limited the use of the gift of prophecy in the church in Corinth:

1Cr 14:29   Let two or three prophets speak, and let the others judge.

He limited the use of prophecy and tongues, requiring an interpreter. He even did not allow women to prophesy in this specific church, probably because there seemed to be an abundance of spiritual gifts in operation. I was once sharing some prophetic dreams with a friend in our church sanctuary. We were both being hunted by a man who seemed to be on a rampage because he had let his wife have an abortion and the fact that we were frequently protesting the abortion clinic right next door to the church drove him to madness. We had to avoid this man (who was living at the church – it was also a homeless shelter). I remembered thinking that I needed to cut off the prophesying of my dreams, but I kept going. This wicked man found us! It was NOT GOOD. So, I have learned to FEAR יְהוָה and not to keep prophesying when it is time to move on! Abba DOES shield the godly from unnecessary trials. Also, in 1 Corinthians 14, we are instructed that '…prophesying is not for unbelievers but for those who believe' (v. 22). So, do not cast your pearls before swine! I have shared prophetic dreams before with unbelievers. Remember, Pharaoh and Nebuchadnezzar were given dreams to bring them to FAITH! In the God of Israel יְהוָה as the one true living GOD!

Back to prophetic excess. If your physical body eats too much, you become obese. If you are feeding on prophetic word too much, you are becoming unbalanced. Prophecy is just one of the gifts that is to operate in a healthy and spiritual body of believers. We need also TEACHING, and others need opportunities to pray and bring revelation that have also received. We need testimonies and other forms of growth. What happens if we become all too dependent on one prophet, is that we are no longer working out our own salvation with fear and trembling…we are just becoming robots and spiritual leeches who remain in spiritual immaturity. I remember sitting under the prophesying of a woman (spiritual mother) who would prophesy out of her home. I was HUNGRY for prophecy having been starved of the spiritual gifts in my

Baptist church upbringing, and would EAGERLY anticipate every Tuesday night! When she prophesied, the atmosphere was electric! People would be delivered from demons by her and when people received the baptism of the Holy Spirit, I was enamored by the power of יְהוָה ! I was only probably 5 years old in Him at that time. Physically, only around 24 years old. I then received a dream in 2007 (of vision) of a huge, overgrown RAT laying on its side, sucking the milk of the mother rat. It had been drunk on too much milk! Abba used this to reveal to me, TOO MUCH OF A GOOD THINGS IS NOT GOOD!

We even have an example from the Old Testament (Tanak).

Zec 13:3   "It shall come to pass [that] if anyone still prophesies, then his father and mother who begot him will say to him, 'You shall not live, because you have spoken lies in the name of יְהוָה.' And his father and mother who begot him shall thrust him through when he prophesies.

Imagine your own parents knifing you if you disobey this commandment! (I know a missionary whose parents attacked him once when he wouldn't shut up.) If you speak 4 prophecies, you are in excess! The lack in most American churches is the fear of יְהוָה. Read Number 24 ... notice Balaam, the FALSE prophet, spoke 4 prophecies (notice also that his prophecies were true). We are to stir up our gifts, use them, and ask יְהוָה for more! Pour out, whether you are an intercessor, evangelist, or prophet. And then come back to the fountain of Living WATERS for refilling so you can pour out again!

Many people who have the gift of prophecy can tend to be 'drama kings' or 'drama queens.' We love attention! We want people to turn their eyes on us. This is why Paul said, 'You can all prophesy one by one so that you all may be encouraged' (1 Cor. 14). If your church meetings become the 'Michael show' or the 'head pastor show,' your congregation is not spiritual. YOU ARE A FAN CLUB! I remembered in the aforementioned home meeting, I would eagerly wait for the woman to speak. She was also physically beautiful, and we have to be on guard to see what our motives are for turning to certain 'prophets.' יְהֹוָה used this woman greatly in my life, but would you believe, this same woman, years later, יְהֹוָה warned me through the writings of Ezekiel. Abba says that He will answer us directly when we reach a level of spiritual maturity.

Eze 14:7 "For anyone of the house of Israel, or of the strangers who dwell in Israel, who separates himself from Me and sets up his idols in his heart and puts before him what causes him to stumble into iniquity, then comes to a prophet to inquire of him concerning Me, I יְהֹוָה will answer him by Myself.

Eze 14:8 "I will set My face against that man and make him a sign and a proverb, and I will cut him off from the midst of My people. Then you shall know that I [am] יְהֹוָה.

Eze 14:9 "And if the prophet is induced to speak anything, I יְהֹוָה have induced that prophet, and I will stretch out My hand against him and destroy him from among My people Israel.

Eze 14:10   "And they shall bear their iniquity; the punishment of the prophet shall be the same as the punishment of the one who inquired…

Yahshua יֵשׁוּעַ said the same thing!

John 16:23   "And in that day you will ask Me nothing. Most assuredly, I say to you, whatever you ask the Father in My name He will give you.

So, I went back to her (disobedience), and the relationship became more and more strained! I realized I needed to wean myself off of her and directly onto Him! You may also realize as you grow that people will begin seeking the gift you have. I found out once that a fatherless believer would be eager to speak to me each week at the Shabbat meeting. Often the prophetic anointing would fall on me, and living waters of prophecy would flow out of my belly, refreshing this brother. I did not realize that he was being spiritually edified as much as he was, until one day, when he said, 'I REALLY ENJOY HEARING YOUR DREAMS AND VISION AND SPIRITUAL REVELATIONS!' There was a fervency in the way he spoke this to me. Bless His name! I was just using my gift.

Whatever side you are on, be it the one edifying others, or the one being edified by a spiritually gifted prophetic person, ask Abba to help you proceed with fear and trembling. You do not want to drain someone more than what they are able to feed you with, nor do you want that to happen to you. Prophesying takes your mental energy, your spiritual strength, and can even physically exhaust you (think of Ezekiel laying on his side for

40 days, or Yahshua יֵשׁוּעַ being nailed to the cross for 6 hours – that was the most prophetic act anyone could have ever done – He is the prophet like Moses that was spoken of in Deuteronomy 18:18). So be on guard against excessive usage!

There is a story in 1 Kings of a younger prophet being deceived by an older prophet. The younger prophet was instructed by our Father not to eat in a place. He was walking in obedience until the older prophet LIED to him about Father telling HIM (the older prophet) that he was to eat. Slowing down to concede to this older prophet cost him his life!

In conclusion - as you grow spiritually, may יְהֹוָה צְבָאוֹת give you GREATER boldness to prophesy, and may you do it with the grace He supplies! I hope this helped you!

Naphtali Services - a ministry that encourages men and women to wrestle with Yah....Call us for prayer 330-354-0448

And please visit our website www.wrestlewithyah.webs.com